LABOUR MARKET POLICIES FOR THE 1990s

ORGANISATION FOR ECONOMIC CO-OPERATION AND DEVELOPMENT

Pursuant to article 1 of the Convention signed in Paris on 14th December 1960, and which came into force on 30th September 1961, the Organisation for Economic Co-operation and Development (OECD) shall promote policies designed:

- to achieve the highest sustainable economic growth and employment and a rising standard of living in Member countries, while maintaining financial stability, and thus to contribute to the development of the world economy;
- to contribute to sound economic expansion in Member as well as non-member countries in the process of economic development; and
- to contribute to the expansion of world trade on a multilateral, non-discriminatory basis in accordance with international obligations.

The original Member countries of the OECD are Austria, Belgium, Canada, Denmark, France, the Federal Republic of Germany, Greece, Iceland, Ireland, Italy, Luxembourg, the Netherlands, Norway, Portugal, Spain, Sweden, Switzerland, Turkey, the United Kingdom and the United States. The following countries became Members subsequently through accession at the dates indicated hereafter: Japan (28th April 1964), Finland (28th January 1969), Australia (7th June 1971) and New Zealand (29th May 1973).

The Socialist Federal Republic of Yugoslavia takes part in some of the work of the OECD (agreement of 28th October 1961).

Publié en français sous le titre:

LE MARCHÉ DU TRAVAIL : QUELLES POLITIQUES POUR LES ANNÉES 90 ?

For almost three decades, the OECD Manpower and Social Affairs Committee has been a proponent of active labour market policies designed to improve the performance of the economy. This message is more important than ever. Treating the social consequences of unemployment is not sufficient. Public policies to encourage job search and to improve skills, competence and motivation will not only increase the individual chance of the unemployed to find a job but will improve the functioning of the labour market generally. Access to gainful work, the equity objective, can thus be husbanded with the reallocation of labour in response to structural change, the efficiency objective.

Many labour market programmes have been pursued in OECD countries to achieve these objectives. However, the results have been mixed and there is an urgent need to take stock of what has been achieved so far. Only on this basis will it be possible to assess what needs to be changed and what policy approaches appear to be the most promising for the future. Desirable reforms may concern the content of particular measures, how they are implemented, and the overall co-ordination and balance between them.

Improving the effectiveness of policies is a gradual process based on learning from experience. Evaluation studies play an important role here but equally useful can be an international comparison and analysis of national policy priorities and resource efforts. This report aims at the latter. It provides a conceptual framework for comparing and analysing labour market policies of OECD countries in an international context. It distinguishes policies in broad terms such as the nature of goals, the principal means and content of public action, and the target groups addressed. A comprehensive empirical review is provided to take stock of current policies followed by the analysis of options and priorities for the future.

Also available

LABOUR MARKET FLEXIBILITY: Trends in Enterprises, by Bernard Brunhes, Jacques Rojot, Wolfram Wassermann (1989)
(81 89 03 1) ISBN 92-64-13286-4 74 pp. £10.00 US$17.00 FF80 DM33

OECD EMPLOYMENT OUTLOOK. JULY 1989
(81 89 02 1) ISBN 92-64-13260-0 226 pp. £23.00 US$40.00 FF190 DM78

NEW TECHNOLOGIES IN THE 1990s: A Socio-economic Strategy (1988)
(81 88 07 1) ISBN 92-64-13180-9 126 pp. £11.00 US$19.00 FF90 DM37

MEASURES TO ASSIST THE LONG-TERM UNEMPLOYED: Recent Experience in some OECD Countries (1988)
(81 88 06 1) ISBN 92-64-13134-5 100 pp. £7.50 US$13.50 FF60 DM26

FLEXIBILITY IN THE LABOUR MARKET. The Current Debate (1986)
(81 86 03 1) ISBN 92-64-12892-1 146 pp. £7.50 US$15.00 FF75 DM33

Prices charged at the OECD Bookshop.

The OECD CATALOGUE OF PUBLICATIONS and supplements will be sent free of charge on request addressed either to OECD Publications Service, 2, rue André-Pascal, 75775 PARIS CEDEX 16, or to the OECD Distributor in your country.

TABLE OF CONTENTS

LIST OF TABLES

CHALLENGES AND OPPORTUNITIES IN THE 1990s

Statement by the
Manpower and Social Affairs Committee on
a new framework for labour market policies
adopted at its 76th session, 4-6 April 1990

The second half of the 1980s has witnessed considerable progress in sustaining economic growth and expanding employment in the OECD area. Progress made in structural reform has contributed to better performance. But persistently high unemployment rates in many OECD countries are an ever present reminder that much remains to be done over a wide range of issues to improve performance and forestall developments that could threaten sustained growth and the achievement of full employment.

Over the longer term, there are both opportunities for, and potential risks to, economic growth and job creation. Pervasive technologies, trade liberalisation and reforms in Eastern and Central Europe have the potential of boosting economic activity globally. On the other hand, three developments pose potential risks to the performance of labour markets:

- Demographic trends will reduce the number of young people entering the labour force – often the most mobile and adaptable. Labour shortages may emerge, adding urgency to policies that mobilise under-utilised human resources.
- With the proliferation of the new technologies jobs generally are becoming more skill-intensive; the very pace of change requires more versatile workers, capable of improving their skills throughout working life. Additional investment in human capital will be required to counter emerging skill gaps.
- In response to growing pressures of structural change jobs will be more varied, in terms of conditions and requirements, and also in the long-term employment and career prospects they offer. Both job search and recruitment are becoming more important and difficult and should be facilitated by policy measures.

The Manpower and Social Affairs Committee endorses the Secretariat Report on a "New Framework for Labour Market Policies" which builds on the principles of an active labour market policy laid down in the 1964 and 1976 Council Recommendations. In the view of the Committee, globalisation results in the increasing interdependence of labour markets and creates a new setting for the conduct of labour market and social policies. The Committee agrees that the challenge for the coming decade will be to focus policy concern on the quantity and the quality of the labour force and the efficiency of the labour market to accommodate economic and social change. This will be crucial to containing the above risks.

Well-designed labour market policies often have the advantage of achieving efficiency and equity objectives simultaneously. While the main policy emphasis will be on the supply side, special demand-side measures for the disadvantaged continue to play a role, in line with the social objectives of labour market policy, as a step towards regular employment. Policies will focus on:

Mobilising Labour Supply

Priority should be given to active measures such as training, placement and rehabilitation programmes for the unemployed, the inactive and those on welfare in order to break dependency cycles, reduce inequality in the access to jobs and generally integrate people into the mainstream of productive activity. These priorities should be reflected in the allocation of resources.

The basic thrust of the notion of the "Active Society" is to foster economic opportunity and activity for everyone in order to combat poverty, dependency and social exclusion. In practical terms, this implies co-ordination of various types of income support to avoid work disincentives, coupled with measures to promote active job search. In order to equalise access to gainful work it is important to make all workers as competitive as possible in the open market. This is particularly important for those drifting into long-term unemployment – often concentrated in economically-depressed regions – whose prolonged detachment from work reduces their employability. Furthermore, the growing interdependence of the global economy and more competition in the labour market will increase the vulnerability of some groups for whom targeted programmes will have to be developed.

The participation of women in the labour market often remains not only below potential but also under-utilised in a qualitative sense, being still too concentrated in low-skilled jobs with only limited career opportunities. Active equal opportunity policies, including measures to facilitate the choices of workers with family responsibilities and child-care needs, should be emphasized and integrated with training and labour market measures aimed at equalising access to gainful work; appropriate provisions in broader policy areas such as education, tax, infrastructure, and social policies will also be needed.

Similarly, measures such as more flexible retirement arrangements and better adapted working environments would increase the participation of others such as the elderly and those with physical, mental and social disabilities whose work potential is often grossly under-utilised. For those with disabilities these arrangements should be co-ordinated with other forms of support, notably with special education and training arrangements.

International migration has historically played an important supply adjustment role in OECD labour markets. Future migration policies – other than those pursued on social and humanitarian grounds – will have to be co-ordinated, in the longer-term perspective, with policies for mobilising and reallocating domestic human resources in both sending and receiving countries. The effective integration of migrants in the society and the labour market of the host countries is an important policy goal.

Developing Employment-related Skills

Avoiding the emergence or widening of a "skill gap" which would have serious consequences for economic performance demands developing new relationships with the education system and reinforcing the key role of the private sector in job training and upskilling of the labour force.

Effective job training depends upon a strong commitment by employers and the co-operation of employees; it also depends upon every worker having acquired a sufficient foundation of general education. Better co-operation between enterprises and education and training institutions will be required to cope with evolving skill requirements and their increasing complexity.

In this context, it is essential that labour market policy be closely co-ordinated with education and training policies, and that an appropriate incentive structure involving employers, employees and disadvantaged groups be put in place to encourage training. The fundamental principles which apply are:

- All young people should complete, before entering the labour market, at least secondary level schooling of sufficient breadth and depth that enables them to take part subsequently in various types of job-related training on a recurrent basis.
- In view of the emerging demographic trends and the continuing pressures to accommodate structural and technological change, particular efforts are required to extend adult training and retraining.
- Public authorities have a role in encouraging the extension and improvement of enterprise training in a broad sense. Governments should act as a catalyst by promoting training co-operation between enterprises and also between enterprises and educational institutions. They can also contribute to improving the transferability of skills by setting standards for curricula and examinations.
- Governments have a special responsibility to ensure that job-related training – constantly adjusted, in close co-operation with the private sector, to rapidly changing skill requirements in the open labour market – is available to the unemployed and disadvantaged groups.

Promoting a Spirit of Active Search

Labour market efficiency should be enhanced by providing a broad range of services to individual labour market participants, be they job-seekers or firms in search of suitable skills; the services should not be limited to short-term objectives but should assist workers in their long-term career development and enterprises in their forward-looking human resource management.

The increasing complexity of the labour market tends to increase "transaction costs" in terms of time and money spent on job search and recruitment. The efficient matching of workers and jobs is therefore crucial. The reallocation of labour to the most productive and rewarding uses is a permanent challenge.

Employment services have a central role to play both in improving the efficiency of the labour market and in equalising access to employment. An efficient information system will depend on its coverage of the labour market. For the majority of job-seekers and employers, the availability of relevant market information will generally suffice. There are, however, many workers who will also need counselling and many enterprises which might benefit from advice on recruitment, manpower planning, human resource development and new organisational arrangements. These will, in future, be an essential element of labour market efficiency.

There is scope for administrative improvement and better co-ordination of different programmes, especially between those for income maintenance, training and employment promotion and placement. It is also important to ensure consistency between services which have short-term effects such as immediate placement, and services which have longer-term effects such as training.

In order to prevent jobless workers who wish to re-enter employment from drifting into long-term unemployment, priority should be given to quick acting market-oriented services such as guidance, and services which increase job motivation, search efforts and job readiness. If these fail, more intensive types of public intervention such as training and employment subsidies should be envisaged.

Close contacts with public authorities, business groups, trade unions and other organisations are important at the local level for the successful delivery of employment services and labour market programmes. These contacts primarily convey direct information about the labour market, but they can also provide a forum for local initiatives, thus mobilising more local resources and hence creating more jobs.

The creation of new enterprises providing additional jobs is a dynamic element in a well functioning labour market. Facilitating self-employment and promoting the necessary entrepreneurial climate and the requisite skills call for co-ordinated policy efforts within government, at central and local level, as well as partnerships between the public and the private sector.

THE POLICY CHALLENGE

Labour market policies operate in the wider context of economic, social, educational and cultural policies. In particular, close interaction between labour market policies and economic policies is essential to ensure the sustained growth of output and employment. Policies which improve the functioning of the labour market, strengthen labour supply and facilitate adjustment to structural change reduce the risk that sustained expansion will be forestalled. Conversely, the more successful macro-economic policies are in maintaining non-inflationary growth of output, the better the prospects for employment and labour market insertion. The fundamental challenge will be to maintain this virtuous circle in the decade ahead.

Labour market authorities, in co-operation with other relevant government agencies and the social partners, will make determined efforts to strengthen labour market policies for the 1990s and beyond, along the lines of the broad framework above. Effective action by the social partners to cope with structural change will reinforce these efforts. The precise contents of national policies will depend upon individual circumstances and institutional arrangements but the common challenges and growing economic interdependence demand that the OECD countries jointly seek viable solutions and coherent policies.

As part of the ongoing work of the OECD on multilateral structural surveillance, the Manpower and Social Affairs Committee will review Member countries' labour market performance within the framework outlined above.

A NEW FRAMEWORK FOR LABOUR MARKET POLICIES

I
INTRODUCTION

In the 1990s the dominant influences on OECD economies are likely to be the rapid and pervasive spread of new technologies and – on the assumption that protectionist tendencies will be overcome – expanding world markets and growing international competition. While this will create new opportunities for growth and prosperity, there are also many risks and challenges ahead. Rapid structural change will have to be accommodated, and adverse demographic trends, i.e. the ageing of the working-age population coupled with strong migration pressures, will impose an additional burden of adjustment on the labour force. Success or failure in coping with these challenges will largely depend on whether labour markets prove to be sufficiently flexible and whether this flexibility can be achieved in a socially acceptable way. Future labour market policies will have to be pursued against this background. They have an important role to play in improving macro-economic performance by augmenting potential growth and removing inflationary bottlenecks. But the reverse relationship is equally important: the success of labour market policies will depend on the general economic climate and a reasonable pace of job-creating growth, hence on the pursuit of appropriate macro-economic policies.

Since its creation in 1961, the history of the Manpower and Social Affairs Committee has been closely linked to the spread of active labour market policies in OECD Member countries. Although the origins of these policies and their evolution varied between countries, there has been a continuum in the pursuit of objectives which centred around three main policy directions:

- To develop human resources and adjust manpower resources to structural changes with a view to fostering economic growth;
- To improve both employability of and opportunities for disadvantaged groups, and thus contribute to social equity;
- To improve the trade-off between inflation and unemployment by stabilizing employment during the cyclical downswing and by removing labour-market bottlenecks during the upswing.

The Committee has devoted its attention to all three concerns, but over the years there have been significant variations in emphasis according to the changing macro-social environment. Among the more formal and "visible‘ pronouncements of the Committee's views were the 1964 Council Recommendation on 'Manpower Policy as a Means for the Promotion of Economic Growth" [OECD (1964)] and the 1976 Council Recommendation on "A General Employment and Manpower Policy" [OECD (1976) Vol.I]. To these could be added the 1980 Declaration on Policies for the Employment of Women [OECD (1980)]and the Communiqués of the meetings of the Committee at Ministerial level in 1982 and 1986, both of which emphasized the need for accelerated job creation and labour adjustment to change.

A critical assessment of the efficacy of labour market policies since 1961 would suggest a mixed record. This was reflected in changing public perceptions of these policies. They were hailed in the 1960s as a way to develop human resources for economic growth and to facilitate adjustment to structural change. They encountered serious problems in the 1970s: while initially welcomed because they were expected to reducc unemployment and poverty, they could not in fact deliver under the prevailing macro-economic circumstances. In the 1980s they were rediscovered as an important micro-economic instrument to remove rigidities and barriers to structural change, but this did not make them particularly popular because it implied a focus on efficiency at the expense of equity. The situation seems likely to change yet again in the 1990s. Labour market policies may be increasingly required to reintegrate the long-term unemployed and other disadvantaged groups into a market which – for demographic and technological reasons – could well be characterised by both shortages of young people and newly emerging skills. Providing opportunities for all to compete in the expanding but rapidly changing economies of the future would revive and strengthen the idea that labour market policies can achieve efficiency and equity objectives simultaneously.

In trying to address the future role of labour market policies this report examines three basic questions: Where have we come from? Where do we stand? Where do we go? These three questions have determined the basic structure of the report. After a brief review of the evolution of labour market policies and the OECD's contribution to monitoring, assessing and fostering these developments (Chapter II), the main body of the report consists of a stocktaking and analysis of labour market policies as currently pursued by OECD countries (Chapter III). This chapter is based on a new data set which permits the measurement of policy inputs such as expenditure on programmes, numbers of staff employed to implement them and numbers of participants. With the help of these indicators, a comparative study is made across OECD countries, focusing on policy priorities, target groups and resource implications. This analysis is followed by an outlook on likely future policy trends in the light of the challenges ahead (Chapter IV). The future-oriented section reviews five broad areas of policy innovation: The Active Society, Education, Women in the Labour Market, Local Development, and Labour Market Efficiency. Chapter V summarises the main points of the report and discusses the framework for future labour market policies.

II

THE OECD AND ACTIVE LABOUR MARKET POLICIES SINCE THE 1960s

The notion of "active manpower policies" used in the past by the OECD reflects a mixed parenthood. The word "active" originated in the Swedish concept of "active labour market policies" as developed in the early 1950s out of frustration with wage restraint policies. The word "manpower" originated in the North American debate of the early 1960s about what to do with "creeping" unemployment of a structural nature which remained unresponsive to general fiscal and monetary stimuli but had to be addressed using "manpower development programmes". It is helpful to distinguish these historical roots and to understand the different approaches on which they are based.

Already, shortly after the war, Sweden was confronted with an unemployment-inflation dilemma: full employment had been achieved through Keynesian demand management but could not be sustained without generating inflation. Wage and price controls, to which the trade union movement initially consented, turned out to be unsustainable. Although central union leaders accepted a wage freeze, this led to wage drift at local level, which was outside the control of the central union leadership, and finally in 1951 to a wage explosion. Hence the search for an alternative solution, initiated and strongly supported by the trade union movement, to prevent the emergence of inflationary bottlenecks. The solution was the concept of an active labour market policy, the basic idea of which was to improve market clearance by selective interventions on the demand side and the supply side but not on the wage-setting process. The role of relative wage adjustments as a market clearing mechanism having thus been diminished, the trade union movement could pursue a "solidaristic wage policy" and reduce wage differentials.

The North American phenomenon of creeping unemployment in the late 1950s and early 1960s, which had no parallel in Europe, was explained in different ways [Ulman (1974)]. For Keynesians, it was mainly the result of maintaining insufficient levels of demand over a prolonged period of time. According to another school of thought, it was due to labour displacements resulting from automation as well as saturation of private consumer demand. Finally, for a third school, creeping unemployment could mainly be explained by growing skill mismatches in the economy. A common element shared by the last two schools was their rejection of general demand stimulation as an effective means to fight unemployment; however, the former group advocated job creation by the public sector (to meet still unfilled community needs) whereas the latter emphasized training and retraining (to remove skill mismatches).

Actual developments in the United States encompassed all three policy proposals: more expansionary demand management was pursued under the strong influence of the

Council of Economic Advisers, and public sector job creation and training measures were introduced with the passage of the Manpower Development and Training Act of 1962. The important difference with Sweden was that the manpower policy package was not part of the macro-economic policy strategy, i.e. manpower policies were not viewed as a possible means to increase the scope for demand stimulation without inflationary consequences. For this, the Council relied largely on price and income policies (wage and price "guideposts"). Manpower policies were mainly confined to public sector job creation and training with a view to assisting disadvantaged groups to reintegrate into the labour market. By contrast, in Sweden the range of labour market instruments was much broader, in accordance with the objective to improve the functioning of the labour market generally and thereby to reduce the inflationary potential of a full-employment policy.

The OECD adopted both components of the concept and added a third one. In addition to improving the inflation-unemployment trade-off and equalising labour market access, the third objective of active manpower policies as promoted by the OECD was to foster economic growth through human resource development. The 1964 OECD Council Recommendation was the principal expression of this comprehensive, three-pronged concept of an active manpower policy. This Recommendation became a vehicle for the Committee to urge Member countries to revise their existing policies or to implement new ones. There were three follow-up reports (1966, 1968 and 1970) on progress made in individual countries in the implementation of the 1964 Recommendation. Detailed country examinations were undertaken under the auspices of the Committee and in close co-operation with the countries concerned. During these years a number of countries profited from these examinations and their detailed preparation by developing comprehensive new legislation and programmes in the labour market area, or by reorganising their administrative machinery for implementing programmes as well as the structure of the public employment and unemployment benefit services.

The 1964 Recommendation offered a menu of options from which countries chose those best suited to their specific or perceived needs. Measures concerning training, placement and job creation for the disadvantaged enjoyed a general boost, whereas the limitations of regional mobility schemes were soon recognised. The OECD had set a collective target of 50 per cent growth of the combined gross national product of its Member countries to be achieved during the decade 1960-1969 [OECD (1962)]. The concept of facilitating manpower adjustment and tapping new sources of labour supply to foster potential growth fitted ideally into this framework.

Although the target was achieved, the optimistic attitude to growth was overtaken by a new concern: in the second half of the 1960s, inflation started to accelerate slowly but steadily. The new tone was set by a seminal OECD Secretariat report of 1970, *Inflation. The Present Problem* [OECD (1970*a*)]. Active manpower policies figured prominently among the various prescriptions proposed by the Secretariat as a means to halt the worsening inflation-unemployment trade-off and to break cycles of "stop - go", which had become prevalent in macro-economic demand management. "Any move towards economic restraint for the sake of disinflation, which can be expected to create unemployment, should be combined from the outset with preparation of selective counter-action. Similarly, any policy move towards overall expansion through general demand management should be combined with measures to facilitate and stimulate appropriate reallocation of resources so as to avoid the emergence of inflationary shortages" [OECD (1970*b*)]. It is not difficult to recognise in this statement the Swedish concept of active labour market policy as it had been developed shortly after the war. In the late 1960s and early 1970s, however, this side of the active manpower policy concept of the OECD gained less ground in actual policy-making than the emphasis on long-term manpower development and adjustment as a means to foster potential growth. Although Sweden extended its capacities so as to be equipped to cater at short notice for 2 per cent of the labour force in training or job-creation schemes [OECD (1972)], and Canada came close to the 2 per cent target, virtually all the other countries preferred as an anti-inflationary strategy to adopt prices and incomes policies. This proved to be an unmitigated failure.

Before creeping inflation in the late 1960s and early 1970s had been brought under control, OECD economies were hit by a quadrupling of prices for imported oil in 1973/74. Governments, concerned by the drop in domestic wealth, initially adopted an accommodating demand management stance which, in the face of unchanged price and wage behaviour, led to a further acceleration of inflation. Hence, in the first place, neither economic policy nor the income formation process (price-fixing and wage-setting) underwent the painful but necessary adjustment to the new international parameters and the shift of economic power to the OPEC countries. The result was a necessary and dramatic policy shift towards severe restraint. But the period of accelerating inflation had lasted so long that inflationary expectations had taken root, and governments were therefore compelled to continue restrictive policies more or less continuously throughout the rest of the decade and beyond. As a result, unemployment rose steadily or remained at persistently high levels. Nevertheless, towards the end of the decade it began to look as if the OECD economies might have turned the corner to a better economic performance. Unfortunately, before they recovered fully from the effects of the first, the OECD economies were hit by the second oil-price shock. This time, however, the necessary adjustments of fiscal and monetary policy to the new parameters occurred more promptly. The result was that, after a severe recessionary period in the early 1980s with steeply rising unemployment, OECD economies – helped by a drop in international oil prices – subsequently experienced a gradual improvement of economic performance (notably with regard to non-inflationary growth, less so with regard to the reduction of unemployment).

The two oil-price shocks changed the thrust of labour market policies quite substantially. Although more and more labour market policies, programmes and new job creation initiatives were introduced and tested during the 1970s, there was less conceptual clarity than in previous periods about what they could and could not achieve. In particular, there was often considerable ambiguity about their potential role in relation to macro-economic demand management.

The first reaction to the recession was to resort to various "bridging" measures which – pending an incipient recovery – would either maintain workers in their current jobs (redundancy-deferring subsidies, short-time working) or would maintain their skills, work attitudes and incomes by placing them in temporary employment schemes in the public sector. When the expected recovery did not materialise, these types of measures soon became discredited. Subsidising employment in existing jobs was regarded as detrimental to structural change, and public sector employment schemes often had the connotation of "make work" arrangements. A new generation of measures was therefore developed emphasizing job creation in the private sector (through incremental employment subsidies) and local initiative programmes, i.e. financial aid or seed money provided to the actors in the local labour market who would then develop programmes on their own initiative responding to local needs and building on indigenous resources.

While these second-generation measures were an improvement compared with earlier efforts, they were little more successful in reducing unemployment. In retrospect it is easy to see that this was impossible as long as the prevailing perception of appropriate macro-economic policy and the actual policy stance was one of restraint. If the overall level of demand for labour is depressed – perhaps as a result of macro-economic policy – job creation initiatives at micro level can only redistribute the incidence of unemployment. To be sure there had been occasional attempts cautiously to reflate the economy and – in line with repeated OECD recommendations – selective labour market measures, mainly incremental employment subsidies, formed part of these reflation packages (German Wage Cost Subsidy of 1974, French Employment Pacts of 1977 to 1980, US New Jobs Tax Credit of 1977-78 and the CETA public sector employment programmes). However, even these timid expansionary initiatives eventually ran up against the inflation and balance-of-payments constraints and had to be abandoned. Nevertheless, for political reasons, labour market programmes usually continued to exist, possibly in a modified form, even after the overall policy direction had changed back to a restrictive stance. It can be said of the 1970s that policy activism prevailed at the micro level, due to pressures on governments in general, and Ministers of Labour in particular, "to do something about unemployment". But this contrasted sharply with policy reticence at the macro level dictated by the underlying economic realities which militated against a more expansionary stance.

The 1976 meeting of Labour Ministers and the adoption by the Council of a Recommendation on "A General Employment and Manpower Policy" bear witness to the political will to find the means to return to full employment without introducing additional inflationary pressures. Ministers discussed and proposed a range of employment-enhancing programmes, but at the same time one could sense a concern that the scope for non-inflationary measures might be limited[1]. Still more expressions of caution emerged from a major report prepared for the OECD by a group of independent experts [OECD (1977*a*)]. While the report stressed the need to pursue job-creation programmes for groups particularly hard hit by the recession as well as for unemployed youth, there was at the same time a clear warning that these programmes should not be run on a scale which would come close to a reflationary policy stance in view of the prevailing inflation, balance of payments and budgetary constraints.

Increasingly, the general view gained ground that if any lasting progress in the return to full employment were to be achieved – other than by prolonged policies of demand restraint forcing wage- and price-setters to modify their behaviour – some fundamental changes in institutions, attitudes, and rules and regulations governing the socio-economic system in general, and the labour market in particular, were required. High and quasi-fixed labour costs, rigid wage-setting procedures, generous social protection, and rules and practices which shielded some workers in secure jobs at the expense of others in unstable jobs, were some of the factors that were perceived as reducing the capacity of national economies to adjust to new international market signals and to profit from new economic opportunities. This led in the late 1970s and 1980s to a long series of OECD policy statements urging micro-economic reforms and ranging from positive adjustment policies, to the need for structural adaptation, to flexibility in product and factor markets and to structural surveillance.

In order to strengthen the social side in this debate the Manpower and Social Affairs Committee initiated conferences on "Social Policies in the 1980s" held in 1980 [OECD (1981)] and on "Employment Growth in the Context of Structural Change" held in 1984 [OECD (1985)]. A report by a group of independent experts on labour flexibility [the Dahrendorf report] was prepared in 1986 [OECD (1986*a*)] together with a technical report by the Secretariat [OECD (1986*b*)]. The Committee met at Ministerial level in 1982 and 1986, meetings at which emphasis was placed on labour market policies to assist structural change and labour market flexibility, and again in 1988, when the focus was on cost-effectiveness in social protection and on the new concept of the "Active Society"[2].

The emphasis in labour market policies on flexibility and adjustment objectives did not meet with general approval. In fact, some observers regarded the focus as biased by employers' interests. However, the deregulation movement also comprised areas like competition policy, price-fixing, procurement practices, where deregulations were clearly directed against the vested interests of business. What was at stake was something more fundamental. It can best be described by the distinction suggested by Dobell (1981). He observes that in the evolution of the welfare state, there was a shift of emphasis from the mere redistribution of income through tax/transfer systems towards direct interventions in the structure of the system which generates income and wealth. The latter aims at altering the distribution of primary incomes (for instance, through minimum wage floors) or the terms on which individuals or enterprises participate in the economic system (for instance, through quantity restrictions on imported goods). This approach, therefore, is designed to alter market mechanisms and to resist (or modify) market signals. The deregulation movement was triggered off by this latter approach of superimposing social goals directly on economic activities. It was not meant to dismantle all regulations, many of which, in fact, are indispensable to make a market economy work.

It remains true nevertheless that many of the deregulations suggested in the labour market area (some of which will be further discussed in the next chapter) implied a serious attack on achieved social standards. The Manpower and Social Affairs Committee has over the years adopted a pragmatic stance and has attempted to steer a middle course between the competing claims for change and for maintaining certain achievements, thus trying to reconcile economic efficiency with social equity. More recently, this has brought labour supply policies such as training, job-search and placement measures back to the centre of the Committee's deliberations. These policies are, of course, not new. But their capacity to meet efficiency and equity objectives simultaneously make them particularly attractive under the present circumstances. They are also best suited to respond to the new macro challenges of demographic and technological change which will affect economic and labour force performance in the next ten years.

III
THE CURRENT SITUATION

To provide an overview of the current pursuit of labour market policies of all OECD countries is an ambitious endeavour. A plethora of approaches, concepts and institutions has emerged over the last decades, especially after the oil-price shocks of the 1970s. Many of these innovative developments in policy-making are difficult to assess as yet. A common perception of "what works" and "what does not seem to work" is only slowly gaining ground, not least because the socio-economic context in which labour market policies have to operate remains in constant flux. This does not detract from the need to take stock of, and critically review, what is happening in order to be prepared to reorient policies to meet the challenges of the future. To take stock is therefore the principal objective of this chapter.

It is useful to distinguish between changes in the regulatory framework of the labour market and labour market programmes. These two areas of policy are often complementary and interactive, and must be considered together in examining the policy effort of a particular country. Yet even this would not cover the whole spectrum of labour market policies, since it does not include indirect policy approaches to affect labour market outcomes such as government efforts to influence collective bargaining or the encouragement of local initiatives and private/public partnerships to improve job creation and local development. Furthermore, the public policy effort would have to be seen in conjunction with the private efforts to achieve certain labour market outcomes, such as collective bargaining over wages and working conditions, or the training provided by private industry. Such a comprehensive overview of a country's total effort to improve labour market outcomes is not the intention in the present report, a point which must be stressed because the expenditure data presented in this chapter do aim at some degree of comprehensiveness and international comparability. It remains nevertheless a partial analysis in that only labour market programmes are included, i.e. only policies which imply the spending of public money. Hence these budget data do not provide a picture of the *entire* effort of a country to influence the operation of the labour market.

In the recent debate on flexibility of product and factor markets, the deregulation of the labour market has attracted particular attention. Yet, as will be shown below, this turned out to be difficult to achieve. At the same time, labour market programmes have become subject to public expenditure constraints. The challenge for the future will therefore be twofold:

i) Sufficient labour market flexibility will have to be achieved within a socially acceptable regulatory framework. Thus, necessary regulations must not stifle innovation and change but prevent an undue burden of adjustment falling on individuals or particular groups. It will be argued (see Chapter IV, section B) that this can best be achieved by internal and external labour market flexibility coexisting and playing a complementary role.

ii) Public expenditure on labour market programmes will have to be reoriented to maximise cost-effectiveness. It will be argued here that priorities should be switched from "passive" to "active" measures, in other words, that policy should be changed from a static concept of income support and protection to a dynamic and future-oriented one of "investing in people".

A. CHANGES OF RULES AND REGULATIONS

Attempts to change rules and regulations have mainly occurred in three areas: wage-setting machinery, employment and redundancy legislation, and working-time arrangements. The first area is only indirectly related to labour adjustment policies; it is directly related to wages and incomes policies which are not the subject of this report. The following section will therefore deal only very briefly with this topic before moving on to the two more relevant areas from the point of view of labour market policy, i.e. employment and redundancy legislation and working-time arrangements.

1. Wage-setting Machinery

Recent attempts to improve the movements of relative wages are typified by developments and trends in countries such as Australia, the Netherlands, Spain, the United Kingdom and the United States where moves have been made (or endorsed by the Administration in the case of the United States) to reform minimum wages, or institute wage-fixing machinery. In Australia, a two-tier wage-fixing system was introduced early in 1987 under which wage increases up to a ceiling of 4 per cent were allowed on the basis of agreements to remove restrictive work and management practices. Developments have subsequently reinforced the trend towards greater decentralisation of wage negotiations and strengthened the linkage to productivity improvements. In the Netherlands, wage bargaining has also been more decentralised and policy at the macro-economic level has ensured a relative lowering of the minimum wage. Since 1986, Spain has not had a central wage agreement based on forecast inflation rates and there has been an increase in establishment-level agreements. In the United Kingdom, the government has attached importance to the drive to encourage more flexibility in pay arrangements in order to allow greater responsiveness to market forces. Among the measures adopted are to give tax relief to encourage profit-related pay schemes and employee share ownership plans, and to reduce the areas within which the remaining Wages Councils operate. These measure were accompanied by more general reforms of industrial relations law and policies to increase competition in product markets. In the United States the Administration has strongly endorsed a two-tier minimum wage structure,with a lower wage rate for new entrants during a temporary training period.

Recent attempts to contain the overall rate of wage inflation are exemplified by Norway and Portugal. The Norwegian government introduced in March 1989, for the second consecutive year, incomes policy legislation to limit hourly wage increases and to freeze dividends in order to curb inflation. Portugal reached wage policy agreements between both sides of industry and the government in 1987 and 1988 to moderate wage increases in the context of a growth policy based on investment. The agreements were based on expected rates of inflation, but whereas the out-turn in 1987 (9.4 per cent) was reasonably close to the forecast (8-9 per cent), the 1988 out-turn of 9.6 per cent was almost double the forecast (5.5-6.5 per cent) and the agreement was abandoned at mid-term. As regards the minimum wage, the definition of the allowances and bonuses to be taken into account was modified in 1987, with the result that the minimum wage declined as a proportion of average wages.

2. Employment and Redundancy Legislation

This is a broad heading. Employment legislation impinges on levels of employment by imposing constraints on employers' freedom to hire and employ labour either directly or indirectly. An example of indirect effects is provided by legislation on working time which lays down that hours worked in excess of specified limits have to be paid at specified rates above the normal rate, with limits set on the amount of overtime that can be worked in a year. Legislation on paid leave entitlements, paid training leave and working ages could also be cited. Examples of direct effects can be found in the legislation still in force in some countries prohibiting certain types of employment for categories of workers, such as young people or women. Another general type of legislation concerns the prohibition of discriminatory practices in the hiring or the employment of workers on grounds of race, gender, colour, or religion (some countries also forbid discrimination on grounds of political belief or social origin).

Redundancy legislation imposes constraints on employers' freedom to discharge workers at will. It may lay down procedures for consultation, the elaboration of social plans, the early warning of the employment service and the payment of indemnities. A general overview of existing legislation on collective and individual dismissals has been provided in an earlier report by the Secretariat on *Flexibility in the Labour Market* [OECD (1986*b*)]. An interesting analysis of economic advantages and disadvantages of employment security and flexible terms and forms of employment has been made by Emerson (1988). The following paragraphs summarise some of the major modifications of legislation in this area, as well as changes in court rulings, new collective bargaining agreements or changes in actual company practice.

Recent work undertaken for the OECD Working Party on Industrial Relations has shown that the traditional concept of "employment at will" in the United States has been eroded in the 1980s by the decisions of the civil courts assessing damages for wrongful dismissal. These decisions included cases which have in effect introduced "the sorts of constraints on an employer's ability to terminate employment which are familiar in other countries with very different legal traditions and histories". The impact of such decisions on employers' behaviour has been to make employers significantly more cautious about the circumstances in which they dismiss workers. Experience in the same period in Canada has been similar.

In addition, in 1988-89, the United States introduced new legislation and amended existing legislation regarding the protection available to redundant workers. The measures involved are the Worker Adjustment and Retraining Notification Act (WARN), the Economic Dislocation and Worker Adjustment Assistance Act (EDWAA), and the Trade Adjustment Assistance programme (TAA). The Department of Labor is consulting with State and local government, business groups, labour unions and public interest groups about the way these measures will be implemented. The first of these measures, WARN, establishes mandatory advance notice requirements in certain cases of plant closings and mass lay-offs: plant closures affecting 50 or more full-time workers by an employer of 100 or more workers would generally trigger advance notice; mass lay-offs affecting at least 500 employees or at least one-third of the workforce and at least 50 employees would also generally require advance notice. Notice must be given to the affected workers or their representatives, the local community, and the state agency charged with assisting dislocated workers. EDWAA revises Title III of the Job Training Partnership Act to provide a new, comprehensive worker adjustment programme for dislocated workers including state rapid response units to assist workers and communities undergoing major plant closing and mass lay-offs, new delivery systems administered primarily at state and local level, labour management committees to assist affected communities, and early referral from unemployment compensation to adjustment services. TAA provides benefits and services for workers displaced from their jobs due to imports. Among the changes introduced are: making training an entitlement; requiring worker participation in training (or a waiver) in order to receive cash allowances; expanded eligibility criteria to include certain oil and gas workers; increased co-ordination with other training and employment programmes; and notification of benefits available to eligible workers through written communications or notices published in newspapers.

In Japan, the courts have developed highly restrictive rules regarding individual dismissals, but the law regarding the rights of individuals in collective dismissals is still evolving. Nevertheless the *practice* of Japanese firms is to regard dismissals as a sign of management failure, even for small firms, "and for an owner-manager of a small firm it is, indeed, a personal failure, more poignant than for the salaried personnel manager of a large corporation" [*Japan at Work*, p. 56, OECD (1989*d*)].

In Germany, the existence of legislation on co-determination means that workers and their representatives are consulted and have legal rights to take part in the decision-making process on a range of issues. This includes issues relating to redundancy. The employer has to inform workers of the introduction of new technical equipment and to discuss with them how they can acquire the technical qualifications enabling them to use the new equipment. In short, the German system relies less than that of most other countries (except Japan) on the external labour market and, as a rule, both law and court decisions require the employer to undertake all reasonable efforts to avoid job terminations. Moreover both special legislation and collective agreements identify special categories of workers who cannot normally be dismissed. These were estimated by C. Buechtemann (1989), in a study of the lessons from an evaluation of the Employment Promotion Act 1985, to number 2.5 million workers in 1985 (excluding public sector workers), more than 13 per cent of employees in employment.

In this context, the Employment Promotion Act of 1985 is seen by the author as an attempt to introduce a moderate amount of deregulation by extending probationary periods during which new employees can be dismissed without legal consequences and by widening the scope for fixed-term contracts, which had been limited by decisions of the Federal Labour Court to cases such as seasonal work, replacement of temporarily absent permanent personnel, helping out in periods of peak demand and carrying out temporary tasks, etc. The new law largely suspended these legal restrictions on the conclusion of fixed-term contracts and firms were able to conclude such contracts in cases where they were uncertain about future labour demand. The study referred to above showed that the impact of the new legislation was modest. Whilst there had been an increase in fixed-term employment over the period from 1984 to 1987, most of the increase had occurred before the new law came into effect. Two out of three firms in the private sector – mostly small and medium-sized firms – had made no use of fixed-term employment in the two years following the introduction of the law. Nevertheless the law has introduced possibilities for increasing the flexibility of working hours and the government has recently decided to extend it until 1995.

In France there was a movement in favour of easing the administrative prerequisites for redundancy through the 1986 legislation, which abolished the need for official consent but introduced an obligation to present "social plans" for redundancies of more than 10 persons by enterprises employing 50 or more workers. The present policy stance, however, is to put the brakes on redundancies by requiring all firms envisaging lay-offs for economic reasons to propose agreements to the workers concerned which stipulate measures for their conversion. The requirements for certain firms to present social plans and to report back to the Works Council on the implementation of the plan and the evolution of the firm's labour force have been strengthened.

In the United Kingdom the trend has clearly been to ease the circumstances in which employers can dismiss workers without risk of being called to account by the courts. Under the Employment Protection (Consolidation) Act 1978, workers were not able to appeal to Industrial Tribunals on the grounds of unfair dismissal if they had been employed by their firm for less than 6 months. In 1980 this period was extended by order to one year's employment and in 1985 it was again extended to two years; these periods were felt to be sufficient to enable an employer to judge whether newly hired workers met requirements. In an attempt to discourage frivolous complaints from being brought before the tribunals, the government has proposed that powers be given to enable the chairmen of tribunals to have "pre-hearing reviews" and to order that either party to a dispute pay a deposit before a full hearing takes place. It has also been proposed that the period after which a discharged employee can demand a written statement of the reasons for dismissal be extended from the present 6 months to two years' employment.

Portugal and Spain are among the countries which have given most attention to expanding the scope for fixed-term contracts in the belief that this enables employers to respond in a cost-effective way to fluctuations in product demand. In Portugal the Supreme Court has ruled, however, that the legislation on fixed-term contracts was unconstitutional, but in Spain fixed-term contracts have applied to the great majority of new hires and are now estimated to apply to roughly a quarter of all employment in Spain.

Finland saw a change in the collective agreement between management and unions in 1988 under which the length of notice was extended in cases of redundancy for economic or production reasons with the aim of providing better opportunities to retain employees and facilitate their transfer to new employment.

3. Working-time Arrangements

Recent developments in working time can be viewed as reflecting a number of apparently contradictory trends. On the one hand, governments want to deregulate so that work can be carried out to meet market requirements. On the other, there is the continuing wish of workers and their representatives to reduce individual working time – but not, however, to reduce earnings in proportion – arguing that this will create employment opportunities for the unemployed. The first trend obviously increases the potential flexibility of labour supply and thus increases the discretionary means of employers to adjust labour inputs to changing market conditions. This trend may also improve equality of access or can be the result of structural changes which make old prohibitions no longer appropriate. Action in this area is mainly through changes in legislation. As regards changes in working time, the impetus is often mainly felt in the collective bargaining process, although in some countries legislation has been introduced or modified.

For example, in Germany a bill on working hours was introduced in 1988 to lay down limits within which the social partners were expected to work out what was required in the particular circumstances of enterprises, such as methods of production, location, etc. In France, too, legislation in 1982 reduced the length of the normal working week from 40 to 39 hours to help increase demand for labour. It was expected that, with the government providing financial aids, moves would then continue towards a goal of a 35-hour week, but in fact progress was sporadic and slower than had been expected by the government of the day. Greece and Spain also reduced working hours through the legislative processes. In Belgium and the Netherlands the governments in the early 1980s negotiated with the social partners so that some future wage increases were translated into reduced working time as part of a work-sharing policy. In the case of Belgium this led to the setting of the 3:5:3 norm under which industrial branches were expected to work out 5 per cent reductions in working time, 3 per cent moderation of pay claims and 3 per cent extra increase in employment. These policies were not as successful as had been expected and initial results turned out not to be long lasting.

The policy of introducing working-time reductions as a means of facilitating an increase in numbers employed was the subject of an enquiry by an OECD evaluation panel, which came to the general conclusion in 1987 that "The position seems to be – and the growing link between the reduction and the rescheduling of working time bears witness to this – that working time reduction is being steadily less regarded as a main weapon in the fight against unemployment. It is increasingly seen as one of the ways of responding to workers' aspirations and one of the tools enabling the labour market to respond to the reorganisation of productive systems for the purpose of avoiding inflation, enhancing competitiveness and hence raising employment."

While a shorter working time will represent a reduction of labour supply of those in the labour market, there are no *a priori* grounds for assuming that total labour supply will be reduced by the same amount. This is mainly because of the willingness of groups which had formerly been outside the labour force to seek jobs with shorter hours. There may well be negative effects on labour costs and productivity, and hence on labour demand as well. It must be noted that it is not only workers, or potential workers, who press for shorter hours. It can be to the advantage of employers, particularly if it helps reduce labour supply without recourse to expensive redundancy procedures, or enlarges the workforce by introducing part-time workers, who tend to be more pliable, less demanding and frequently are more poorly compensated than full-time workers.

Part-time working has increased in many countries, partly spontaneously, i.e. without any change in the legislative framework. This seems to be the case for Australia, Canada, Ireland, Japan, Sweden, Switzerland, the United Kingdom and the United States. Countries such as Belgium, Portugal and Spain have taken action to stimulate the growth of part-time employment. Belgium has made it possible for persons who are unemployed to take part-time jobs and receive part-time unemployment benefit, and has stressed the importance of such employment as an alternative to complete unemployment; the other two countries have extended the legal possibilities of contracts for part-time work. Greece is in the unusual position of not recognising the existence of part-time work in its legislation.

Another group in the labour force which has become more significant in many countries, partly as a result of government action, partly as a consequence of the change in demand for labour, consists of persons working on temporary or fixed-term contracts. Some of these workers would prefer to have indefinite-term employment; but a proportion, particularly in the younger age groups, may not seek such a continuing relationship: they may appreciate the possibilities of varied experience without the long-term commitment associated with traditional contracts. For employers one of the advantages is that they can try out workers over fixed periods without incurring obligations and expenses, if they decide not to keep them at the end of this time. Belgium, Germany, Portugal and Spain have taken action to facilitate the conclusion of fixed-term or temporary employment contracts, at least in specific circumstances. One way in which some countries have helped encourage the spread of temporary work has been by the creation of special branches of the Public Employment Service dealing only with temporary work. Belgium and the Netherlands have taken this approach.

Early retirement has been used to try to create employment opportunities for the unemployed by allowing older workers to move into retirement (or partial retirement) before the normal pensionable age. It has sometimes proved of doubtful utility and sometimes led public authorities to incur heavy financial commitments from which there is no escape. There appears to be more interest now in reversing this approach and allowing older workers to continue in employment after reaching pensionable age, increasing their pension entitlements. Germany, however, has recently introduced a measure to promote early partial retirement with aid towards the expenses incurred if an unemployed person is engaged to make good the time not worked by the early retiree. Other countries retain early retirement as a means of slimming down the labour force in industries facing structural adjustment problems (in the steel industry in Italy, for example).

B. LABOUR MARKET PROGRAMMES

Labour market programmes are normally publicly financed. This makes it possible to measure the policy input in quantitative terms and to compare the size of the inputs between different categories of programmes, both nationally and internationally. With this objective in mind, the Secretariat, in close co-operation with Member countries, has developed a new internationally comparable data set on public expenditure for labour market programmes. The first results of this work have already been published in the two most recent *OECD Employment Outlooks*. Further results on expenditure are presented here, as well as additional internationally comparable policy indicators: staff resources used in the conduct of labour market programmes as a further input indicator, and programme participants as a policy output indicator.

This material is presented in two steps. First, in this section, the data set is used for a discussion, programme by programme, of the main instruments of active labour market policy. The discussion also draws on other recent work such as the results of the Manpower Measures Evaluation Panels and the section is arranged according to four main programme areas of active labour market policy: the Public Employment Service, labour market training and youth measures, subsidised employment and measures for the disabled. Secondly, the material is used in section C for a comparative analysis of national policy packages, i.e. the varying emphasis placed on the different programme categories and the size of the overall labour market expenditure in Member countries. Methodological details about the data, and the choice of programme categories which had to be made to make this new data set internationally comparable, are provided in the Methodological and Statistical Annex.

1. The Public Employment Service

The Public Employment Service (PES) is a public agency delivering various services including information, placement and counselling. Frequently it is also in charge of the payments of unemployment compensation and the implementation of a range of other labour market programmes. A public employment office is a local branch of such an agency.

In all OECD countries except Belgium, Switzerland and the United States, the PES is run by central public authorities. At central and sometimes also at regional and local level, most Public Employment Services have some kind of tripartite management or advisory bodies on which, in addition to public authorities, the trade unions and employers are represented. In Canada, Germany, Norway and Sweden, these perform functions comparable to those of a supervisory board, a model that Ireland and the Netherlands have also recently adopted. In Australia, Belgium, Finland and Spain, the Labour Ministries maintain a direct management responsibility, though there are elements of tripartism in most of these countries, too. The United Kingdom has recently abandoned a tripartite management system.

In the United States, the 1933 Wagner-Peyser Act provides that the federal government pays Employment Service grants to states for a statutory set of activities. States may choose which of these authorised activities they will perform. Individual states may also be reimbursed for the costs of various other services, such as providing national labour market information under separate contracts with the federal government.

The roles actually played by the PES vary according to both institutional factors and the range of functions in its remit, as well as with the size of its staff and other resources. The following sub-sections examine these aspects of PES networks.

The market share of public placement operations

Labour market information and placement services can be provided by both private and public agencies. Private employment agencies are especially common in the United States and widespread also in several other countries; but their role is largely complementary, with a concentration in certain sectors of the labour market and in large cities. Their overall impact may therefore, even in the United States, be moderate compared with the PES. In most countries the private agencies are subject to regulation, which may for instance confine their activities to temporary jobs or certain occupations. In a few countries including Austria, Germany and Sweden, profit-making institutions for placement are forbidden with only minor exceptions.

Policies to encourage private placement activities have proved useful in some situations, notably in connection with industrial restructuring. Enterprises often find it in their interest to facilitate transition of redundant workers to new jobs. Japanese firms frequently make extensive efforts of this nature, sometimes with support from the government, as do some employers in other countries. It has become increasingly common for employers to engage fee-charging agencies for what is sometimes called "out-placement" to handle redundancies. Employers may also co-operate with local communities and other *ad hoc* bodies which provide placement services on a non-profit basis. The PES may support such initiatives, as is done for instance in Canada with a scheme called Industrial Adjustment Assistance.

But when job-losers fail to find work immediately, they are normally obliged to register with a public agency in order to receive unemployment benefits. Then, if not before, the public authorities have a principal responsibility for assisting in job search and placement so as to minimise the duration of joblessness and financial support. It has, however, seldom been considered desirable for public agencies to concentrate only on the unemployed – an approach which might diminish the status of these agencies in the eyes of employers. This is the main reason why many governments restrict private employment services: if allowed, they might focus on the most attractive workers. Even where private agencies are not restricted, the PES will usually attempt (and in principle is expected) to cover as large a part of the labour market as possible. Nonetheless, this ambition is often thwarted in practice by high unemployment and by resource limitations.

One indicator measuring the coverage of PES services is the proportion of all job openings that are notified to it. In various surveys made during the 1980s, this "market share" has been estimated to be in the range of 1/10 to 1/3 in several countries, and as high as 2/3 in Sweden[3]. But little is known about how many of the notified jobs are actually taken up by workers receiving information via this channel. The proportions mentioned can therefore be regarded as maximum estimates of the quantitative role played by employment agencies in recruitment. Newspapers and personal contacts are probably at least as important as sources of job information[4].

The high share of vacancies notified to Swedish employment offices is due to legislation making such notification obligatory for employers. Similar laws exist in Belgium, France and Italy, too, though apparently with less effect, and also in Spain. Italy to some extent requires employers to hire workers from official waiting lists (*chiamata numerica*), a regulation that has recently been somewhat relaxed, though not abolished. In other countries there are few formal prescriptions for employers about how to advertise vacancies and recruit workers.

In some cases informal practices exist whereby the placement officers send only one person to each notified job vacancy. This may merely imply that the services provided for employers include selection of suitable candidates. But it may also reflect a policy on the part of the authorities to place relatively difficult cases first. Such "negative selection" runs the risk of being self-defeating, however, because employers may lose confidence in agencies which do not provide adequate information about all job-seekers. One possible solution to this dilemma is for the PES to negotiate with employers about jobs for some proportion of hard-to-place persons in combination with others who are subject to positive selection.

The PES may also help job-seekers more indirectly by helping them to solve problems themselves. Job-search courses and similar forms of intensified counselling are increasingly common (see below). Furthermore, PES authorities are deeply involved in training. Some recent administrative reforms, notably in Australia, Ireland, Portugal and the United Kingdom, have specifically aimed to strengthen connections between employment services and training. But labour market training is not an alternative to work; it is a means to make it possible. At least in part, its effectiveness depends on the quality of the labour market information on which individual training decisions can be based. Greater responsibility for training will therefore enhance the need for the PES to be well informed about the job market. Monopoly or not, it remains a crucial objective of the PES to maximise the coverage of its vacancy information.

Implementation and administration of programmes other than placement services

The PES network in most countries is used as the delivery system for a range of programmes. When these consist of simple grants and subsidies to employers or job-seekers they usually form part of, or are used as a means of enhancing, the basic placement activity. Programmes requiring more complex administration of their own (such as institutional training, direct job creation and rehabilitation of the disabled) are more often managed by separate bodies; but employment agencies may still take part in their planning and in assigning individuals. There are also examples of labour market-related programmes handled entirely by specialised agencies.

Programme activities create an administrative workload which, if carried by the employment agencies, will divert resources from their basic services. Much of this administration is usually centralised at headquarters or in specialised offices, implying that staff have been removed from day-to-day contact with job-seekers and employers. Decisions to admit individuals to a particular programme must, however, be based on judgement about individual circumstances which can only be made at a decentralised level.

The administration of unemployment benefit systems tends to absorb large resources – sometimes so much so that it dominates placement-related activities. In Belgium, France, Ireland and the Netherlands, unemployment benefit systems are administered entirely by separate organisations, a model which has sometimes been regarded as advantageous because it permits employment offices to concentrate on placement. But such a separation may also render the administration of unemployment compensation less efficient from the point of view of labour market policy. A key requirement for benefit payments is precisely that the jobless seek work, and this may be difficult to enforce – other than in a formal or perfunctory manner – unless there are strong ties with the placement function. Germany, Japan and Spain have a single agency for both placement and unemployment compensation. The same holds true of many other countries, although there are often separate bodies for some parts of the benefit administration. The United Kingdom started a major organisational reform in 1987 with the purpose of integrating the unemployment benefit organisation with the PES, a process now completed at central and regional level, but still underway at local level. An independent organisation will deliver training services with a strong element of local planning and leadership from employers.

The size of staff and other resources

PES activities are often labour-intensive, in particular when priority is given to serving those with difficulties in finding jobs. Such placement efforts have to be based on individual contacts with job-seekers and employers. To illustrate the capacity to serve individuals, the first three columns of Table 1 show the numbers of service points in a number of OECD countries, as well as the average number of staff. Although most of the work is done in employment offices, there are also often some smaller auxiliary units as indicated for some countries in the third column. The average size of an employment office, including auxiliary units within its area, is between 8 and 20 employees in most countries; it is substantially higher in Germany and also higher in Belgium, Denmark and the Netherlands (the second column of Table 1). The averages conceal much variation within countries: most office

Table 1. **Structure of employment office networks**

Country (year)	Number of employment offices	Average staff per employment office	Number of smaller units	Number of regional headquarters
Australia (88-89)	337	15	—	30
Austria (88)	111	15	—	9
Belgium (87)	116	40	—	30
Canada (88-89)	573	9	224[a]	15
Denmark (88)	28	76	150	14
Finland (88)	180	12	—	13
France (86)	685	13	1 000[b]	22
Germany (88)	146	180[c]	485	9
Greece (88)	100	8	120	7
Ireland (88)	48	6	—	8
Japan (89)	479	..	120	..
Netherlands (89)	65	56	75	30
New Zealand (89)	72	8	—	6
Norway (89)	108	15	—	18
Portugal (87)	59	16	—	5
Spain (87)	606	7	—	52
Sweden (89)	330	16	60	24
Switzerland (88)	26	6	3 000[d]	26
Turkey (89)	108	15-20	—	12
United Kingdom (89)	1 759	19	405	9
United States (88)	1 800	..	..	..

a) 104 campus offices, 67 agricultural offices, and 53 itinerant and casual offices.
b) Municipal authorities performing limited employment office functions such as registering unemployed persons.
c) Excluding separate departments for administration of unemployment benefits and network and programme management.
d) Municipal offices.
Source: National submissions to the OECD.

networks include both large offices with over 100 employees and some quite small ones. But full-service offices usually need to have some minimum size; thus where there are units with just one or two staff members, they usually have only auxiliary status.

Table 2 shows the total staff numbers for employment offices and other parts of the labour market administration, including that for unemployment benefits. The first column shows the employment office personnel, which in most cases corresponds roughly to the number of staff involved in placement and counselling, as well as related support functions. It also includes some staff with other tasks; thus certain administrative functions in employment offices cannot be meaningfully isolated, because they are normally done by the same persons as those responsible for placement and counselling. Germany may be regarded as an exception, since its offices are relatively large on average and have extensive administrative functions in separate departments. Therefore, only staff involved in placement and counselling plus some support functions have been included in column 1 for Germany.

The second column of Table 2 shows the number of staff engaged in other than client-related activities, including most of the administration of labour market programmes. These

Table 2. **Staff of public employment services and related administrations**

Country (year)	Employment offices[a] [1]	Network and programme management[b] [2]	Employment offices plus network and programme management (Col. 1 + 2) [3]	Unemployment benefit administration (when separate) [4]	Total including unemployment benefit administration (Col. 3 + 4) [5]
Australia (88-89)	5 000	4 300	9 300	3 141	12 400
Austria (88)	1 649	817	2 466	1 191	3 657
Belgium (87)	..	..	5 324	..	..
Canada (88-89)	4 920	7 862	12 782	8 780	21 562
Denmark (88)	2 125	681	2 806	..	..
Finland (88)	2 100	600	2 700	..	..
France (87)	9 000	11 000[c]	20 000	11 450	31 450
Germany (88)	26 200	13 400[d]	39 600	17 600	57 200
Greece (88)	..	..	840	1 600	2 440
Ireland (88)	300	575	875	1 624	2 500
Netherlands (89)	3 660	610	4 270	9 000	13 270
New Zealand (89)	550	250	800	1 250	2 050
Norway (89)	1 570	700	2 270	75	2 345
Portugal (87)	970	1 186	2 156	—	2 156
Spain (87)	4 000	..	..	—	..
Sweden (89)	5 188	2 264	7 452	260	7 712
Switzerland (87)	1 500	4	1 504	442	2 000
Turkey (89)	..	..	2 200	—	2 200
United Kingdom (89)	32 732	15 800[e]	48 500	—	48 500

a) Including internal support functions and local administration (except for Germany—see Note *d)* below).
b) Mainly central and regional headquarters of employment agencies. Staff who implement programmes, such as teachers and work supervisors, are generally not included.
c) Regional and central offices of the national employment agency (ANPE) plus the Labour Ministry's administration in each *département (services extérieurs du Travail et de l'Emploi).*
d) For Germany, staff with administrative functions within employment offices are included in columns 2 and 4, and not in column 1. About 4 000 staff trainees are included.
e) Including the Training Agency (which manages programmes) but excluding the Skills Training Agency (which provides courses).
Source: See Table 1.

figures correspond essentially to the staff in regional and central offices – except for Germany, where the figure also includes parts of local office staff. With regard to such programmes as training and job-creation, it should be noted that the figures in general only cover staff deployed in administration, not in the delivery of services. Thus, with minor exceptions, they do not cover teachers in training programmes or supervisors in job-creation schemes. Administrative staff engaged in unemployment compensation are shown in column 4 – to the extent that the offices do not deal with placement. Column 5 gives the grand total.

In absolute terms, the total staff figures are quite large for several countries – almost 60 000 in Germany and close to 50 000 in the United Kingdom (including Training Agency staff). However, the proportion of staff engaged in placement and other directly employment-related services to clients is often small. Sometimes it is below 30 per cent, as in Canada, France, Ireland and the Netherlands, where more staff are responsible for paying out unemployment benefits than for helping the unemployed find jobs. The general administration and programme management also consume large resources. A notable exception is Switzerland, where most of the network consists of small municipal offices.

Relating the total number of PES and administrative staff to a country's working-age population shows a typical ratio of about one officer per 1 000 persons of working age. There are relatively small variations between countries, although the variation is somewhat greater if only local office staff are considered (Table 3). Another indicator relates the number of staff to the numbers of jobless people – the prime target group of the PES, though not the only one. As the first column of Table 4 reveals, in several countries each placement officer is facing an average backlog of more than 200 unemployed job-seekers. Country differences are more pronounced here. Sweden, for instance, has a ratio of only 14 unemployed persons for every placement officer.

Two further issues have to be taken into account in connection with resource considerations: methods of service delivery and the use of computers. Most employment offices have adopted some form of self-service based on easy access to vacancy information. According to a recent OECD evaluation panel, self-service is attractive to many job-seekers and also cost-effective, because some people can find jobs for themselves. In 1984, self-service was the main form of employment-office activity in Australia, the Netherlands and the United Kingdom. Elsewhere, a majority of clients usually received some personal advice, even

Table 3. **Staff of public employment services per thousand of working-age population (15-64)**

Country	Employment offices	Employment offices plus network and programme management	Total including unemployment benefit administration
Sweden	1.0	1.4	1.4
United Kingdom	0.9	1.3	1.3
Germany	0.6	0.9	1.3
Denmark	0.6	0.8	..
Norway	0.6	0.8	0.9
Finland	0.6	0.8	..
Australia	0.5	0.8	1.1
Belgium	..	0.8	..
Netherlands	0.4	0.4	1.3
Canada	0.3	0.7	1.2
Austria	0.3	0.5	0.7
Switzerland	0.3	0.3	0.4
France	0.2	0.5	0.9
New Zealand	0.2	0.4	0.9
Spain	0.2	..	..
Portugal	0.2	0.3	0.3
Ireland	0.1	0.4	1.2
Greece	..	0.1	0.4
Turkey	..	0.1	0.1

Source: See Table 1.

Table 4. **Average number of unemployed persons per staff member in public employment services in 1988**

Country	Unemployed persons[a] per staff member in: Employment offices	Employment offices plus network and programme management	Employment services including unemployment benefit administration
Sweden	14	10	9
Switzerland	15	15	11
United Kingdom[b]	53	36	36
Finland	55	43	..
Norway[b]	68	47	46
Austria	74	49	33
Denmark	81	61	..
Germany	86	57	39
Australia	109	58	44
Belgium	..	80	..
Netherlands	152	131	42
New Zealand	175	120	47
Canada	213	82	49
Portugal	266	120	120
France	271	122	78
Spain	713	..	..
Ireland	733	251	88
Greece	..	360	124
Turkey	..	1 380	1 380

a) Standardized unemployment data, mostly based on labour force surveys rather than PES registers.
b) 1989.
Source: Table 1.

though they used self-service facilities as well. Some governments have taken the opportunity to cut the number of placement staff; others have found that the problems faced by most unemployed people nevertheless call for individual attention.

Vacancy registers are now computerised in almost all OECD countries. Usually there are also computerised registers of job-seekers, intended for placement purposes, unlike the unemployment benefit registers. Several agencies have automatic search procedures and routines for matching workers to jobs. The most important advantage is that this speeds up the display of vacancies and so less time is needed to fill them. Thus computerised information can greatly improve the services; but, like the self-service methods, it may not reduce staff requirements very much except in relation to workers with only minor employment problems. The potential for saving personnel may be greater in connection with administrative functions, including in particular the running of unemployment benefit systems. Given the current size of benefit administrations, more modern data-processing and other efforts at rationalisation might provide a way of releasing many employees who could perhaps be more usefully employed in the placement services.

Job-search courses and other intensified counselling

Provision of employment services can be described as a set of Chinese boxes. In countries where the vacancy information is available in full, with the names of employers given, the first visit of a job-seeker to the PES may involve only a receptionist who provides the relevant vacancy list. If this does not suffice, the job-seeker may ask for a talk with a placement officer who can contact employers. The next step, which might take place "further back in the office" with more specialised staff, consists of counselling about alternative strategies such as intensive job search, training or measures to overcome disability. Finally, some unemployed people need so much advice and support that it can hardly be given within the ordinary framework of an employment office. This has led to the introduction of special group activities, usually lasting one or more weeks. These can take different forms and have varying names. Sometimes they focus on self-help, like the "job clubs" in Australia, France and the United Kingdom, the Canadian "job finding clubs", the Dutch "application clubs" and the Austrian "help-yourself groups". Alternatively, training centres may provide short courses with a similar purpose, like the Irish "job search courses" and the Danish "labour market introduction" courses. Facilities for rehabilitation of the disabled, such as the "labour market institutes" in Norway and Sweden, can sometimes be used for the same purpose.

Currently the long-term unemployed constitute the main target group for the latter type of in-depth measures. In many countries, the PES has adopted special procedures to make sure that all long-term unemployed persons are called to interviews and urged actively to address their problems. These procedures, too, have various names: "Newstart" (Australia), "Restart" (Netherlands, United Kingdom), or "13th-month interview" (France). In most cases they are obligatory after a given duration of unemployment. Other particular groups may also need out-reach programmes: school drop-outs, inner-city youth, ethnic minorities, women re-entering the labour market. As a principle, targeted counselling and remotivation to strengthen job search always appears justified when there is a risk that certain persons will lose contact with the labour market. But in the end, the basic priority problem for the PES is to ensure a well-balanced distribution of its combined resources, including the services available to everybody, and the general enforcement of the job-search requirement for all persons receiving unemployment benefits.

Mobility support

The PES usually has some funds at its disposal for helping the unemployed to take up jobs in other localities. Such support can take many forms, as for instance in Germany within the framework of a programme called "measures to promote the taking up of jobs". Elsewhere the support is more strictly confined to travel and removal costs. Travel costs can often be paid both in connection with interviews and when the jobs are to begin. Some countries provide an extra financial incentive on top of merely reimbursing the costs incurred by the individual.

An OECD evaluation panel on measures for displaced workers found that help with removal expenses had not proved very useful as a means to promote mobility. The number of workers applying was usually low. The panel concluded, with reference mainly to experience from Canada, Sweden and the United States, that a large incentive must be offered to persuade workers to move. On the other hand, the modest incentives under study did appear cost-effective to the extent that they were actually used. The same evaluation panel observed that local governments in depressed regions tend to fear that outward mobility will have a negative impact on these regions. The region may suffer in terms of effective demand when unemployed people move out. Furthermore, the chances of future improvement in a regional economy may depend partly on the local availability of labour. However, as far as the PES is concerned, the main objective is to help individuals to take vacant jobs, wherever these happen to be; regional objectives appear to be better pursued by other means.

2. Training and Youth Measures

The role of training in labour market policy

Job training is more than an attempt to find a solution to temporary employment problems; it is also an investment for the future. Yet it will be of little avail unless it actually leads to work. Training programmes must therefore reflect both short-term and long-term considerations. Differing priorities placed on these two perspectives have given rise to a wide range of programmes and policies adopted in OECD countries. A selective and remedial approach dominated labour market training for more than two decades. Many of the largest training programmes currently run by labour market authorities are of this nature. They address specific difficulties facing job-seekers and employers, but they do not attempt to provide all the skills a workforce needs. In other words, they are alternatives neither to public action in the field of general and vocational education in schools nor to initiatives by employers to provide training on the job.

The principal target groups under this approach are the unemployed and those at risk of losing their jobs. In the United States, priority is also given to other economically and educationally disadvantaged persons. In some countries, including Canada, Germany, the Netherlands and the United Kingdom, recent changes have strengthened the focus placed on the unemployed, and especially the long-term unemployed. Additional objectives are often pursued as well, however, as for instance those of relieving "bottlenecks" in the economy, helping women into jobs dominated by men, and promoting certain technologies.

Elsewhere, however, training programmes have much broader functions. In a number of countries the labour market authorities are strongly involved in training which is either not targeted on any particular group of workers or targeted only in a very loose general sense. Frequently the objective is simply to improve the competitiveness of a country's workforce as a whole, or large parts of it, or to address long-standing deficiencies in the existing system of education and training. Where such broad aims are predominant, the treatment of job training as an element of labour market policy, and hence its distinction from other forms of vocational education and training, has lost some or even much of its meaning. However, because this report is concerned with labour market policy, it cannot deal with these issues from the standpoint of training policy in the broad sense, which would have to encompass the whole spectrum of school-based and enterprise-based training. (Some of these broader aspects are discussed in Chapter IV, section B.)

Four main groups of training or training-related programmes are examined here. They can all be viewed as forming part of the package and concept of labour market policy prevailing in the OECD countries. The first two groups are programmes directed at adults (or all ages, with adults dominating). These two groups taken together make up the programme category Labour Market Training. The other two groups of programmes, which for the most part can also be viewed as some form of training, make up the category Youth Measures. The two sub-groups used here refer to whether the adult training and youth programmes are selective and mainly targeted on the unemployed, or whether they are more generally available.

Training for unemployed adults

Training of jobless adults has long been a major strand of labour market policy in countries such as Austria, Canada, Finland, France, Germany, Norway and Sweden; and it has recently become so in Australia and the United Kingdom. Workers are admitted to these programmes after individual assessment of what training they need in order to become permanently employed or re-employed. The costs of these programmes are usually borne entirely by the government. In most countries – the United States is an exception – the cost is dominated by subsistence allowances paid to the trainees. These often correspond to, or slightly exceed, the level of unemployment benefits.

Table 5 shows the size of most such programmes by numbers of participants and the public outlays incurred. The programmes are open to unemployed adults who encounter

Table 5. **Training for unemployed adults and those at risk**

Country	Participants starting per year as percentage of the labour force	Average duration in months	Public outlays: Total as percentage of GDP	Public outlays: US $ per starting participant[a]	Public outlays: Outlay per participant as percentage of average income[b]
Australia	0.4	3	0.02	1 500	10
Austria	0.9	3	0.07	2 700	16
Belgium	1.6	..	0.13	3 000	19
Canada	1.1	6	0.22	7 000	37
Denmark	1.4	7	0.23	6 500	31
Finland	1.2	6	0.27	8 800	42
France	2.3	2.5	0.28	4 600	27
Germany	1.5	8	0.25	7 200	37
Greece	0.1	4.5	0.02	3 150	60
Ireland	1.4	3	0.40	6 800	77
Netherlands	2.3	4	0.20	3 500	22
New Zealand	4.4	4	0.50	3 000	24
Norway	2.7	2.5	0.29	4 500	20
Portugal	0.1	..	0.01	2 400	60
Spain	1.2	2	0.09	1 600	20
Sweden	1.7	5	0.54	12 000	60
Switzerland	0.3	..	0.01	2 800	10
Turkey	0.3	..	..	..	..
United Kingdom	1.4	..	0.22	5 000	31
United States:					
Dept. of Labor	1.0	3.5	0.05	1 800	9
Total including "Perkins Act"[c]	6.4	..	0.11	650	3

a) The conversion to United States dollars has been made using average 1988 exchange rates.
b) Average income: annual GDP per capita.
c) See the Annex table for the United States, note *e)*.
Source: See Annex. The data refer to calendar year 1988 with the following exceptions: Spain (1987), Australia, Sweden and the United States (1987-88), Canada (1988-89), the Netherlands and Norway (1989) and the United Kingdom (1989-90).

difficulties in finding suitable jobs, although in some countries the training capacity may be used for other purposes as well.

In most of the countries shown in Table 5, the bulk of training takes place in special centres controlled more or less directly by labour market authorities. The courses are usually shorter and more focused than, for instance, the kind of training offered to young people. In many countries the training can also take place in other public or private institutions or in enterprises. Often, as for instance in the Netherlands, New Zealand and Sweden, the employment offices can in principle finance training in almost any institution, provided that it serves the specified purposes in each individual case. But specialised training centres nonetheless play the central role.

Only in one country – Denmark – has enterprise-based training hitherto represented the main option. The United Kingdom has recently introduced a scheme, called Employment Training, which includes large amounts of training in enterprises for unemployed people. Elsewhere, too, company-based training is often used for this group though on a smaller scale, as for instance in Austria, Canada, Germany, the Netherlands and the United States. Sometimes public authorities subsidise such training in the same way as they fund training in other institutions; but more often they pay wage subsidies for trainees who are being hired by the employers concerned. In France, Spain and Sweden firms can receive subsidies for training tenured employees who are threatened by lay-offs, especially in connection with restructuring.

Before the results of Table 5 are discussed, it is important to make some technical points concerning this and the following tables. For the number of participants the most frequently available and reliable figure is the number of persons starting training during the reference year. A similar measure would be the number of participants who have completed a course during the year, thereby excluding drop-outs. Both these flow data can be viewed as measuring annual throughput. A different kind of measure is the average number of participants at any point in time.

Annual public spending divided by the number of persons starting (columns 4 and 5 of Table 5) measures, approximately, the amount of public money invested in each trainee. With a given amount of total spending, a high ratio indicates that the money is concentrated on a few individuals, implying relatively long or otherwise expensive training, whereas a low ratio indicates that the money is spread more thinly over many individuals who receive relatively short or less intensive training. However, this approximation depends crucially on two factors. It will be less accurate if training courses are fairly long (which generally is not the case) and if the training volume is changing rapidly over time (which is often the case). In technical terms, it can be said that the ratio is the more reliable for making comparisons between programmes and countries, the more the underlying inflow and outflow correspond to a steady state.

Table 5 has been designed to permit simultaneous consideration of different kinds of information about training. The data must be used with caution. But taken together, participant numbers (column 1), the average duration of training (column 2), spending as a proportion of GDP (column 3) and the average expenditure per participant (columns 4 and 5) should give a rough impression of the size of these training efforts. As the table shows, many countries provide training of this type for between 1 and 2 per cent of the labour force every year. Such training typically lasts between 2 and 6 months and costs the government between 2 000 and 8 000 U.S. dollars per trainee, including subsistence allowances and course expenses.

Start and duration data can also be used to calculate the average participation in training at any point in time. This average participation can be more readily compared with average stock data of people in employment or unemployment. It indicates to what extent unemployment has been reduced by putting people into training programmes. Table 5 shows, for example, that in New Zealand 4.4 per cent of the labour force were in training for one-third of the year; hence training had a short-term relief effect on New Zealand's unemployment rate of about 1.5 percentage points. Similar calculations show about 1 percentage point for Germany and between 0.5 to 1 percentage points for Canada, Denmark, Finland, France, the Netherlands and Sweden.

But the main employment effect should, of course, occur after people have finished training. According to follow-up studies carried out in Finland, Germany, Ireland, Sweden and the United States, the proportion of ex-trainees finding jobs soon afterwards is often in the order of 70 to 80 per cent[5]. Unfortunately, little is known about how many of these people would have obtained work without training, how long they have remained in their jobs and whether they have displaced other job-seekers in finding work.

Compared with total unemployment, the training effort appears modest in most countries. However, this observation has to be seen in relation to available job openings. Training for the unemployed should generally aim at well-identified vacancies which they can take up when they are trained for them. It is possible, in some countries, that low numbers of suitable job vacancies have for some time represented an effective constraint on training efforts.

According to an OECD evaluation panel, a focus on skill shortages is crucial for success. It has been found, for example, that some of the less favourable job-placement results reported in Australia (Labour Adjustment Training Arrangements) and the United States (certain applications under the Job Training Partnership Act, Title III) were due to a poor match between the training provided and the actual skill profiles in demand. The Swedish Labour Market Board reported [AMS (1989)] that in 1988, when there were widespread skill shortages that could be met by training, 72 per cent of those finishing courses found jobs within six months. In 1983, by contrast, only 60 per cent of trainees had found jobs six months later, because then the courses could not be sufficiently focused due to a much lower number of vacant skilled jobs.

On-the-job training may provide a less costly alternative to courses in training centres. It also has the advantage of ensuring direct contact with the labour market: once a person has been accepted for on-the-job training with an employer, he or she tends to have a significant chance of getting a permanent job. Thus an OECD evaluation panel, referring mainly to North American experience, found that on-the-job training was on average more useful than classroom training. Some countries have also recently taken action to increase the involvement of enterprises in training for the unemployed, as for instance Australia, Canada, the Netherlands and the United Kingdom.

Despite the merits of on-the-job training, however, it may not prove sufficient to replace all kinds of institutional training which are currently offered for workers with employment problems. There is considerable variation as to how experienced employers are in providing training. Some kinds of training are also inherently difficult to organise in enterprises. This is apparently an important reason why countries with large training programmes for unemployed people usually rely heavily on institutional training. Furthermore, many in-firm training schemes include some minimum requirement of training which must be provided off-the-job.

The quality of training, especially in enterprises, often suffers from an inadequate institutional "infrastructure" for training, such as traditions among teachers, documented teaching methods, commonly accepted skill definitions and skill certification. Several of the programmes mentioned, including notably that of the United Kingdom, involve major efforts to establish such infrastructures. Elsewhere, as will be shown, similar concerns have led to initiatives to regulate or support the training of employed adults in general.

Training for employed adults

It is not possible in the context of this framework for labour market policy to take account of all public and private provisions for adult training. This sub-section does, however, make a few observations concerning general efforts to upgrade the adult labour force, followed by some facts about the most important public programmes in which OECD governments promote labour market-related training for adults in general, i.e. other than the programmes for the unemployed treated in the previous sub-section.

It must be kept in mind that most of the training given within enterprises is not subsidised. In most countries it is not regulated by the government. One result is that there are few reliable data about such training. In a few countries, however, there is public regulation of enterprise-funded training. In France, for instance, employers are required to spend at least 1.2 per cent of their payroll costs for staff training. According to official records the relevant expenses in 1987 amounted to 2.51 per cent of French employers' payroll costs, or about twice the legal minimum [CEREQ (1989)]. In Germany, curriculum and examination issues are extensively regulated by specialised bodies, but these have little control over the quantity of training or the amounts of money employers spend. In Ireland, the labour market authorities manage a compulsory levy/grant scheme covering certain industries, including most of manufacturing. Irish enterprises must spend between 1 and 1.25 per cent of their payroll costs either for training or for paying levies which the authorities then spend on promoting training in enterprises.

In many countries, including the three mentioned above, part of employers' expenses for adult training are used collectively by several employers or by employers and trade unions together. In some countries, including Austria and Germany, and more recently Ireland and Portugal, the government supports some such co-operative facilities; but often they are run with little or no public support.

International comparison is complicated by the widely different ways in which education and training systems are organised, in both the public and private sectors. In some countries, notably Japan and the United States, probably the most important approach in public policy regarding adults is to provide an efficient market framework for private providers of training. This is facilitated by the existence in these countries of relatively uniform high school systems – although the quality of schools may differ – which most adults have attended. Their university sectors have become gradually more diversified, to attract many categories of adults, as they have also in several other countries. But in Europe and Australia, such a broad use of university-type institutions is hindered by the fact that the vast majority of adults are not eligible for study at post-secondary level, despite recent expansion of secondary-school attendance. Instead, several countries have introduced more specialised public institutions for recurrent training of adults, such as the Australian Technical and Further Education (TAFE). These institutions provide training essentially at secondary level, for both labour market and more general purposes.

Within the European Community, the Social Fund currently provides financial incentives for governments to adopt a range of job-related measures, with training in a very wide sense as the predominant aim. The Fund has recently spent 3 billion ECUs per year, a sum which is soon to be doubled. The biggest part is spent in the less affluent regions. Persons under 25 years old are intended to benefit from 75 per cent of the Fund's spending; but within this age group the Fund does not require that the supported programmes are targeted on any particular category. In effect, the Social Fund is being used to a large extent for programmes included in Tables 5 to 8. But the Fund also subsidises many other projects which are selected on a discretionary basis, especially for training that takes place in particular enterprises.

The most important government programmes in favour of job-related non-targeted training for adults are listed in Table 6. These programmes are quite disparate in nature, but almost all are managed by labour market authorities. Denmark stands out as giving high priority to a network of public training centres, which offer mainly short courses (1-3 weeks) for employed persons. These courses are designed to train unskilled and semiskilled workers. Each year Danish employers release a considerable proportion of their least skilled employees for such training. Canada, Germany, Greece, Ireland, Japan and Portugal offer somewhat longer training for employed persons, both in training centres and in enterprises. The Greek and Portuguese programmes are currently in a process of expansion, with significant resources (including European Community Funds) devoted to investment in new training centres. Canada, France, Ireland, Japan, the Netherlands, Sweden and the United Kingdom have schemes in which enterprises can get support for more specific training purposes such as the introduction of new technologies. Many of the above-mentioned

Table 6. **Training for employed adults**

Country	Participants starting per year as percentage of the labour force	Public outlays		
		Total as percentage of GDP	US $ per starting participant[a]	Outlay per participant as percentage of average income[b]
Australia	0.04	0.01	4 600	33
Belgium	0.1	—	2 900	19
Canada[c]	0.6	0.04	2 300	12
Denmark	5.5	0.24	1 600	8
France	1.6	0.04	1 000	6
Germany	0.8	0.07	3 500	18
Greece	0.5	0.20	5 000	95
Ireland	1.6	0.21	3 000	36
Japan[d]	0.9	0.02	1 000	4
Portugal[e]	0.5	0.11	1 950	49
Spain[f]	0.1	—	600	7
Sweden	0.5	0.02	1 250	6
Turkey	3.0	..	..	..
United Kingdom[g]	0.4	0.01	400	3

a) The conversion to United States dollars has been made using average 1988 exchange rates.
b) Average income: annual GDP per capita.
c) The programme entitled "Skill shortages". "Innovations" is not included.
d) Excluding promotion of technological change.
e) Excluding training other than that in centres.
f) Training for new technologies. Certain other measures are not included.
g) Only training grants to enterprises are included.
Source: See Annex. The data refer to calendar year 1988 with the following exceptions: Belgium, Denmark, Ireland and Spain (1987); Australia and Sweden (1987-88); Canada and Japan (1988-89); the United Kingdom (1989-90).

programmes for training unemployed people (Table 5) can also be used to some extent for the kind of purposes considered here.

Training for young people

A relatively narrow definition of "youth measures" has been adopted here, focusing on measures to promote the transition from school to work – especially in age groups that broadly correspond to upper-secondary education. This definition excludes most cases in which comparatively young people take part in programmes available for any age group. Some inconsistencies are, however, almost inevitable in the classification of programmes[6].

As regards most of the special youth programmes, in the narrow sense, any analysis of their social and economic functions must be undertaken primarily against the background of each country's education system. For one thing participation in upper-secondary education is still relatively low in some countries, while elsewhere it is close to 100 per cent. At the upper-secondary level, certain countries have large apprenticeship systems while others rely much more on full-time school education. This will be discussed further in Chapter IV, section B. To illustrate these differences, Table 18 shows the proportion of 17-year-olds who are enrolled in education. A distinction is made between full-time and part-time education; the latter type is offered essentially to apprentices, who spend the rest of the time in enterprises.

Countries with lower-than-average upper-secondary school participation include Australia, New Zealand, the United Kingdom and several Southern European countries. To improve the employment situation of young people, these countries effectively have the choice between two alternative strategies. One option is to promote an increase in the proportion of young people attending general upper-secondary education – possibly reaching the high proportions typical of Japan and North America. The other option is significantly to increase and develop enterprise-based training along the lines of the apprenticeship systems in Austria, Germany and Switzerland.

Upper-secondary school participation has indeed been increased substantially during the 1980s in Australia and some European countries. But most European school systems are structurally very different from those of Japan and the United States, implying that solutions to youth problems may have to be different too, unless the education systems are fundamentally changed. In particular, upper-secondary schools in Europe, with few exceptions, maintain a deeper split between general and vocational tracks. Policy strategies in Europe – as in the United States – have to some extent been designed to strengthen the theoretical elements of education along both tracks. But equally often, European governments have been concerned with shortcomings affecting the relationships between education and the labour market, and this has led them to rely on labour market authorities to provide new activities in the area of vocational training, especially enterprise-based training[7].

Table 7 lists the most important programmes in support of apprenticeship and related forms of enterprise-based vocational training and work-practice schemes. While many of these programmes were introduced in response to youth unemployment, they are not exclusively limited to unemployed young people or other categories of disadvantaged youth: they are open to any young person who is interested, subject only in some cases to educational requirements. Practically all the participants are placed in enterprises, but there are often elements of classroom training in the schemes.

All programmes in Table 7 except the German "dual" apprenticeship system are managed by labour market authorities. This German scheme is included in the table for

Table 7. **Support for apprenticeship and related forms of general youth training**

Country	Participants starting per year as percentage of the labour force	Public outlays		
		Total as percentage of GDP	US $ per starting participant[a]	Outlay per participant as percentage of average income[b]
Australia	0.8	0.04	1 600	11
Finland	0.1	0.01	3 200	15
France	2.9	0.19	2 500	15
Germany[c]	0.5	0.01	1 100	6
	[2.1]	[0.42]	[8 500]	[43]
Greece	0.3	0.04	1 800	35
Ireland	0.6	0.09	3 700	42
Italy[d]	0.7	0.23	10 800	82
Netherlands	0.8	0.05	2 600	17
New Zealand	0.5	0.01	400	4
Portugal	0.1	0.05	2 900	74
Spain[e]	0.04	0.02	11 800	149
Turkey	0.7	0.04	240	18
United Kingdom	1.4	0.22	5 100	32
United States	0.1	—	140	1

a) The conversion to United States dollars has been made using average 1988 exchange rates.
b) Average income: annual GDP per capita.
c) The main German figures refer to apprentice allowances paid in certain cases; the figures within square brackets represent the entire apprenticeship system (see text).
d) Only employment-training contracts; apprenticeship subsidies not included.
e) Excluding work experience for students.
Source: See Annex. The data refer to calendar year 1988 with the following exceptions: Italy and Spain (1987); Australia, New Zealand and the United States (1987-88); the Netherlands (1989); the United Kingdom (1989-90).

comparison; as already indicated, it has to some extent served as a model for labour market programmes in other countries – although in Germany it is normally regarded as forming part of the education system rather than of labour market policy. The German system has undergone significant reforms during the last decade. Its school-based parts have been extended, and now account for one to two days per week. The practical training for which employers are responsible has also been upgraded, partly with public support; it now takes place to a larger extent than before in special training workshops and other institutions, sometimes run collectively by groups of enterprises within a particular industry. Thus the proportion of training time devoted to ordinary work has declined.

The "dual" nature of modern apprenticeship systems, with training taking place partly in schools and partly in enterprises, is inherent in a majority of the schemes listed in the table. Most of the schemes therefore differ from the traditional type of apprenticeship, which still exists in several countries, although with less public support and regulation. Usually, the governments' financial involvement has focused on measures to improve the quality of training, such as stricter curriculum enforcement and more classroom instruction. Nevertheless, the extent and nature of actual training activities differ widely – both between and within programmes. In countries with high youth unemployment, public policy-makers inevitably are particularly concerned with the need to increase the number of trainees, and this goal is not always easily reconciled with that of controlling quality.

Apprenticeship training in North America is not quite comparable to that in Europe. The average age in North America may be as high as 24 years, and access often depends on job tenure within the occupation concerned (notably in construction). Hence, the North American schemes can almost be viewed as training for employed adults, rather than initial training for labour market entrants as in Europe. The apprenticeship support of the United States has been included in Table 7; that of Canada, by contrast, does not form a separate programme but is part of the programmes mentioned in Tables 5, 6 and 8, depending on the eligibility criterion used for each individual trainee.

Programmes for unemployed or disadvantaged youth

Table 8 shows programmes targeted on unemployed or disadvantaged youth. Their content varies relatively widely – from augmented support to encourage enrolment in normal education or apprenticeship training to special courses of remedial education in basic skills and various forms of work-practice schemes.

Table 8. **Measures for unemployed or disadvantaged youth**

Country	Participants starting per year as percentage of the labour force	Public outlays		
		Total as percentage of GDP	US $ per starting participant[a]	Outlay per participant as percentage of average income[b]
Australia[c]	0.2	0.01	1 850	13
Austria	0.3	0.01	1 500	9
Canada	0.6	0.02	1 200	6
Denmark	1.8	0.24	4 900	25
Finland	0.4	0.02	2 000	9
France	1.4	0.06	1 800	11
Germany	0.4	0.04	4 200	21
Ireland	2.4	0.33	3 300	37
Netherlands	0.2	0.03	4 500	28
Norway[d]	0.5	0.09	6 900	31
Portugal	0.4	0.06	1 400	35
Spain[e]	1.7	0.18	2 300	29
Sweden[f]	0.6	0.09	5 800	29
United Kingdom	0.02	0.01	7 300	46
United States	0.6	0.03	1 800	9

a) The conversion to United States dollars has been made using average 1988 exchange rates.
b) Average income: annual GDP per capita.
c) Excluding the Community Youth Support Scheme.
d) Excluding wage subsidies.
e) Excluding subsidised work experience.
f) Including only the "youth teams".
Source: See Annex. The data refer to calendar year 1988 with the following exceptions: Denmark and Spain (1987); Australia, Sweden and the United States (1987-88); Canada (1988-89); Netherlands and Norway (1989); the United Kingdom (1989-90).

Because unemployment tends to be highest among those with poor education, the first policy priority is often simply to discourage young people from dropping out of school and to encourage them to return to regular education and training. Some countries such as Australia and Sweden have restricted or abolished the right of those under 18 years old to obtain unemployment benefits. The Netherlands, several Nordic countries and Ireland have experimented with "job guarantees" for young people; these involve provision for direct job creation, but they also require that all possibilities of education and training must be carefully considered.

Australia, Austria, Denmark, Germany, Ireland and Sweden all offer special support to unemployed young people who enter regular forms of education or training. Other programmes in the table are mainly designed to provide the young unemployed with work practice. Significant programmes of the latter type exist in Australia, Canada, Denmark, Finland, France, Ireland, the Netherlands, Norway, Spain and Sweden. Normally, the work includes some form of training, although it may not always be very extensive.

Many training programmes for unemployed people or for adults in general (Tables 5 and 6) can also be used to some extent by youth. In addition, the youngest groups of adults – aged 20-29 – tend to be highly represented in most kinds of adult training, regardless of how the target groups are defined.

3. Subsidised Employment

This section will focus on programmes which selectively promote employment for the unemployed (or a sub-category, such as the long-term unemployed) and other groups with employment handicaps. Three types of programmes will be highlighted: subsidies for regular employment in the private sector, support for unemployed persons who start enterprises, and direct job creation in the public sector.

Financial incentives to stimulate employment can take other forms as well, such as an across-the-board reduction of payroll taxes (notably social security charges) to increase labour demand or a reduction of marginal income tax rates to strengthen labour supply. These measures alter the cost and income structure of the economy. Because of their pervasive nature and macro-economic ramifications they are not included here as labour market programmes. Also not included are employment subsidies which form part of regional development policies. These measures usually imply a grant or across-the-board exemption from payroll taxes within certain geographical areas, or they are tied to specific investment projects. The following section will, however, cover a small number of regional subsidies targeted on special groups of workers.

Another type of programme not covered here consists of financial support to enterprises in crisis. Such measures cannot be viewed as labour market programmes unless they focus on the employment of individual workers rather than on keeping companies afloat. Saving jobs is often nevertheless an indirect target. It is worth noting that the cost per worker of rescuing bankrupt companies has sometimes proved very high compared with ordinary labour market programmes. To avoid confusion of policy objectives it must be determined whether government is responsible for particular enterprises, as distinct from employment. This may of course differ from case to case. But if a plant closure is inevitable, the best policy is usually to facilitate it. For employers, various social measures may be attractive to "buy off" redundant workers. Public authorities, too, have often concentrated much of their attention on this function: their efforts in such cases tend to be dominated by income maintenance programmes for redistribution of income. But clearly, it would be better if the redundant workers could be helped to find new jobs.

Subsidies to regular employment in the private sector

Incremental employment subsidies can be targeted on special groups or non-targeted, i.e. available to all employers who increase their workforce above a certain baseline (for instance, 90 or 100 per cent of the actual number of workers currently on payroll). Since 1988 Spain has had a non-targeted subsidy, consisting of deductions from taxable income accorded in proportion to the increases in employment[8]. From time to time in the past Canada, Sweden, the United Kingdom and the United States have used non-targeted schemes but have since abandoned them.

At present, the great majority of schemes in force are targeted employment subsidies. They are usually temporary, and most of them are paid in connection with recruitment, normally on condition that other workers employed by the company are not dismissed at the same time. Some subsidies are used for other purposes such as to prevent lay-offs. Table 9 lists the most important targeted subsidies.

A majority of countries favour the long-term unemployed. Finland, Germany, the Netherlands, Portugal and Sweden offer on average about $3 000 or more per long-term unemployed person recruited. Other countries pay significantly lower amounts but have a higher take-up (e.g. Australia and Greece).

Some subsidy schemes are targeted on relatively broad and varied groups of workers. The United States' Targeted Tax Credit is available for hiring nine different groups of adults and youngsters, including especially those receiving various kinds of income support. Subsidies to encourage recruitment of older workers play a significant role in some countries, notably Germany, Japan and Spain. Other targets of subsidies include part-time work (France) and jobs with relatively low pay (the Netherlands). Several countries support local initiatives for the creation of permanent jobs for the unemployed; but these programmes are usually small and only those of France and Portugal make up significant parts of the figures in the table. Japan focuses a number of measures on the prevention of unemployment in depressed industries.

The sums in dollars per worker shown in the table represent average accumulated subsidy payments per participant. They are paid over varying periods, typically four, six or twelve months. Sometimes there are several variants, as in the Netherlands where there is one subsidy lasting six months, paid to persons unemployed for over a year, and another one lasting up to four years for those out of work for more than three years.

The cost per participant in a subsidy programme is about as high, on average, as the cost per participant in a training programme (Table 5). In Australia, where the subsidy has a relatively high take-up, training programmes instead play a more modest role for unemployed adults. In some other countries the main option for this group consists of on-the-job training grants which may in effect be quite similar to recruitment subsidies. The big Danish scheme listed in Table 5, for example, is largely an instrument for work insertion although it also requires employers to provide training. The same may be true for parts of the Canadian Jobs Strategy.

Some countries which do not appear with large schemes in Table 9, such as France, Italy and Spain, have extensive programmes of a similar nature but which focus specifically on training and work practice for youth (Tables 7 and 8).

Evaluation studies have shown that most recruitment subsidies carry a heavy deadweight, i.e. many subsidised jobs would have been created anyway. Often only about 20 per

Table 9. **Subsidies to regular jobs in the private sector**

Country	Participants as a percentage of the labour force		Public outlays		
	Persons starting per year	Average stock	Total as percentage of GDP	US $ per starting participant[a]	US $ per participant place and year[a]
Australia	0.6	0.2	0.04	1 900	5 900
Finland	0.4	0.1	0.03	4 100	12 200
France[b]	0.2	..	0.01	1 900	..
Germany[c]	0.2	0.1	0.02	5 900	8 700
Greece	1.0	..	0.13	1 800	..
Ireland	0.2	0.1	0.01	1 400	2 600
Netherlands	0.3	0.4	0.04	5 300	4 000
New Zealand	..	0.7	0.21	..	8 500
Norway	..	0.08	0.02	..	13 400
Portugal	0.1	..	0.04	3 100	..
Spain	0.1	..	0.02	3 250	..
Sweden[c]	0.4	0.1	0.04	4 600	13 700
United States	0.5	..	0.01	500	..

a) The conversion to United States dollars has been made with average 1988 exchange rates.
b) Some measures are excluded.
c) Subsidies to construction during the winter are excluded.
Source: See Annex. The data refer to calendar year 1988 with the following exceptions: Germany, New Zealand and Spain (1987); Australia, Sweden and the United States (1987-88); Finland, the Netherlands and Norway (1989).

cent of subsidised jobs are created as a result of the schemes. Hence the programmes are much more expensive in relation to their quantitative net effect than is suggested by the amount spent per worker. An OECD evaluation panel, studying measures for the long-term unemployed, concluded that the main effect of recruitment subsidies is the advantage they give to targeted persons compared with other job-seekers [OECD (1988*a*)]. Such a redistribution of job opportunities may be justified, especially when some people have difficulties so great that they might otherwise never become employed.

Subsidies to unemployed persons starting enterprises

A majority of Member countries provide financial support to unemployed persons who start their own business and work as self-employed. The largest such schemes can be found in France, Greece, Ireland, Spain and the United Kingdom (Table 10).

Historically these subsidies have been regarded as extensions to unemployment benefit programmes. In some countries (Belgium, Luxembourg, Portugal, Spain and demonstration projects in the United States) they consist of unemployment benefits paid as a lump sum or during some fixed period, often augmented with grants or loans. But more frequently they constitute separate programmes with similar subsidy amounts. In only a few countries (e.g. Spain and the United States) does the drawing of benefits to start an enterprise deprive the entrepreneur of future unemployment compensation if the business fails. In Australia,

Table 10. **Subsidies to unemployed persons starting enterprises**

Country	Participants starting per year as percentage of the labour force	Public outlays	
		Total as percentage of GDP	US $ per starting participant[a]
Australia	0.01	—	1600
Belgium	0.04	..	..
Denmark	0.03	0.02	26000
Finland	0.14	0.03	8800
France	0.23	0.03	5350
Germany	0.04	—	2900
Greece	0.29	0.05	2100
Ireland[b]	0.21	0.03	3000
Portugal	0.10	0.02	1500
Spain	0.45	0.20	9100
Sweden	0.04	0.01	7100
United Kingdom	0.28	0.04	4200

a) The conversion to United States dollars has been made using average 1988 exchange rates.
b) Excluding the "Community Enterprise" programme.
Source: See Annex. The data refer to calendar year 1988 with the following exceptions: Germany and Spain (1987); Australia and Sweden (1987-88); the United Kingdom (1989-90).

Denmark and Finland, the authorities offer special training for unemployed persons who contemplate starting a business.

Evaluation studies in France and the United Kingdom have shown that between 50 and 60 per cent of participants remain in business for over three years. British evaluations also suggested that about one-quarter of the surviving enterprises would not have been started without support. Hence a sustained net effect may be in the order of 15 per cent of total participation [OECD (1989*c*)]. Surviving enterprises may have hired additional workers, which is not reflected in these data.

Though part of labour market policy, these programmes are also a sub-set of policies to promote business and industrial development in general. Problems facing new entrepreneurs and small businesses are addressed by governments in several other ways which fall outside the scope of this report. Perhaps most importantly, measures to increase access to the regular capital market – where most of the funding takes place anyway – may reduce the need for subsidies.

Direct job creation in the public sector

Before the mid-1980s a relatively large part of labour market budgets was spent on special public employment programmes for the unemployed. These programmes were temporary and not meant to compete with regular employment. The workers were assigned by the PES for limited periods on the assumption that the works would be interrupted as soon as the labour market improved.

In the 1930s, several governments pursued large investment projects to employ the jobless. Public works of this type still exist; but most of the recent direct job-creation efforts have concentrated on service jobs or maintenance of local infrastructure. This change in content occurred partly because construction had become too capital-intensive, but also because of changes in the skill composition of the unemployed.

According to Table 11, the largest programme for direct job creation is currently run in Belgium. It differs from most such programmes, including older Belgian ones, in that its participants are given regular employment contracts, usually with local authorities. Other forms of public recruitment have been restricted in Belgium so that in effect a large part of all public sector job opportunities are earmarked for the unemployed.

Countries with significant temporary-work programmes are Finland, Germany, Ireland, Portugal, Spain and Sweden. In Germany and Ireland the individual work assignments typically last almost one year; elsewhere they are usually shorter.

Australia, the Netherlands, New Zealand and Norway phased out most of their direct job creation during the latter half of the 1980s. The United States did so already before 1985, while the United Kingdom's Community Programme has been superseded by the Employment Training programme in 1988. These changes were not motivated by improvements in the labour market but by a widespread belief that the unemployed were not well served by direct job-creation measures of this kind. Concern with poor efficiency and cost control was also important for these decisions.

In most programmes the works are organised by local bodies but financed by central government. An OECD evaluation panel found that administrative problems often impaired efficiency. This was partly due to frequent changes of the rules. But there were

Table 11. **Direct job creation (public or non-profit)**

Country	Participants as percentage of the labour force		Public outlays		
	Persons starting per year	Average stock	Total as percentage of GDP	US $ per starting participant[a]	US $ per participant place and year[a]
Australia[b]	0.1	0.1	0.02	4900	10900
Austria	0.1	..	0.02	9450	..
Belgium	..	1.8	0.67	..	12900
Canada	0.2	..	0.02	3800	..
Finland	2.6	1.1	0.44	6800	16400
France	0.2	0.1	0.01	2200	4700
Germany	0.5	0.5	0.16	13800	14800
Greece	0.4	..	0.02	650	..
Ireland	0.8	0.8	0.24	7300	7000
Netherlands	0.1	0.1	0.03	9100	9600
Norway	..	0.3	0.14	..	21000
Portugal	0.4	..	0.05	1300	..
Spain	2.1	..	0.12	1300	..
Sweden	0.8	0.3	0.17	7800	18600
United States	0.1	0.1	0.01	3700	5100

a) The conversion to United States dollars has been made using average 1988 exchange rates.
b) Measures for Aboriginals.
Source: See Annex. The data refer to calendar year 1988 with the following exceptions: Belgium and Spain (1987); Australia, Sweden and the United States (1987-88); Canada (1988-89); the Netherlands and Norway (1989).

also basic conflicts of objectives among the bodies involved: local communities were primarily concerned with the outcome of the works rather than with employment. They tended to regard the programmes as merely a source of finance for community projects which otherwise they would have to finance from local revenues. It is possible, therefore, that efficiency would benefit if these grants were strictly related to the wages of workers selected by the local public employment office.

In efforts to improve efficiency, policy-makers have also tried to combine work with more structured activities designed to enhance employability and job search. For example, when Norway introduced a new programme in 1989 in response to rising unemployment, it stipulated that the work assignments must be interrupted by periods of job search or training every four weeks.

The OECD evaluation panel found that direct job creation can improve the future job chances of participants to some extent. This positive effect did not, however, seem very large. Furthermore, it was not clear whether the effect had any strong relation to the content of the works. Some participants obviously would have needed more full-fledged training; but the work experience might also be useful in itself, if only by reducing the risk of some people becoming entirely alienated from the life of work.

4. Measures for the Disabled

The notion of disability as used here denotes physical, mental and social factors which represent obstacles to employment. The programme category covers activities designed specifically for this group. But like youth programmes, this programme category corresponds only approximately to a particular clientele. Disabled people participate in other labour market programmes, too. Sometimes they make up large proportions in all programmes – especially perhaps when unemployment is relatively low, as in the Nordic countries. Any labour market programme may include some specific features to integrate disabled participants. Training centres, for instance, may organise special introductory courses in order to bring disabled persons into their mainstream activities. Such efforts are included in the tables discussed above.

Thus the size of special measures for the disabled (Tables 12 and 13) does not measure the total policy effort for this group. Canada, Ireland and Italy have no such special programmes at all, and in some other countries they are quite small. Where they are large, "disability" may simply have been broadly defined. Swedish rehabilitation centres, for instance, receive many whose handicaps are social in nature and which may sometimes merely consist of the fact of having been unemployed for a long time.

Most governments require medical certification of eligibility for some of the programmes. Sometimes, as in Austria and the Netherlands, the procedures are connected with social security provisions; alternatively the PES may consult medical specialists of its own. But even where strictly medical criteria are used, it is hardly possible to separate the medical judgements entirely from labour market conditions. It must be recognised, for instance, that some physical ailments cause more problems in labour markets dominated by heavy manufacturing or forestry than they do where many service jobs are available.

The largest rehabilitation programmes in terms of public spending are those of Denmark and Germany, followed by programmes in Finland, Sweden, Switzerland and the United States (Tables 12 and 14). New Zealand's rehabilitation programme has the highest number of participants, but its spending per person is relatively low.

Table 12. **Vocational rehabilitation of the disabled**

Country	Participants starting per year as percentage of the labour force	Public outlays	
		Total as percentage of GDP	US $ per starting participant[a]
Australia	0.1	0.01	4 900
Austria	0.3	0.02	2 200
Denmark	1.4	0.13	3 800
Finland	0.5	0.04	3 000
Germany	0.7	0.12	7 400
Greece	0.02	0.01	7 100
New Zealand	1.4	0.02	250
Portugal	0.1	0.03	3 400
Sweden[b]	0.5	0.09	7 100
Turkey	0.05	0.004	250
United Kingdom	0.06	0.01	3 000
United States	0.7	0.04	2 100

a) The conversion to United States dollars has been made using average 1988 exchange rates.
b) Excluding workplace adjustment.
Source: See Annex. The data refer to calendar year 1988 with the following exceptions: New Zealand (1986-87); Denmark and Germany (1987); Australia and the United States (1987-88); Sweden (1988-89); the United Kingdom (1989-90).

Table 13. **Work for the disabled**

Country	Average stock of participants as percentage of the labour force	Public outlays		
		Total in per cent of GDP	US $ per participant place and year[a]	Outlay per participant place as percentage of average income[b]
Denmark	0.6	0.13	8 700	41
Finland	0.2	0.07	13 800	72
France	0.3	0.05	5 900	39
Germany[c]	0.3	0.07	9 000	45
Netherlands	1.3	0.69	20 400	132
Norway	0.4	0.18	16 900	76
Sweden	1.7	0.67	14 800	73
Switzerland	0.6	0.04	4 100	15
United Kingdom	0.1	0.02	10 000	62

a) The conversion to United States dollars has been made using average 1988 exchange rates.
b) Average income: GDP per capita.
c) Excluding measures for seriously disabled persons.
Source: See Annex. The data refer to calendar year 1988 with the following exceptions: France (1986); Finland (1987); Sweden (1987-88); the United Kingdom (1989-90); Norway (1990).

Many of these activities take place in dedicated centres. For disabled individuals, the stay in such a centre often starts with a test to determine what work they can do and what special arrangements might be needed to make work places suitable. This may last one or several weeks. Another important activity consists of adjustment courses for particular handicaps, often including training in the use of mechanical and electronic aids. After this may follow a more vocationally-oriented course. As already indicated, this often takes place in ordinary training centres, but it may also be wholly or partly provided within a rehabilitation organisation.

The employment of the disabled, like that of unemployed people in general, can be promoted with both subsidies to regular jobs and direct job creation. But the cost per person is often higher, and sometimes the individual assignments last much longer as indicated by the term "sheltered work".

The relatively biggest work programmes are those of the Netherlands and Sweden followed by Denmark, Switzerland, Norway, Germany, France and Finland (Table 13). These countries have large networks of sheltered workshops run by local or regional bodies. Costs are high, although the workshops are expected to market their products commercially. The average Dutch or Swedish workshop shows a net operating loss in excess of the entire wage bill. Those employed often stay on for many years. Policy-makers have frequently stated that sheltered work should lead to placement in the regular labour market, but in this respect the rate of success is low. Sweden also has a large programme of wage subsidies for disabled persons in the regular labour market. Designed to provide an alternative to sheltered work, the subsidy can last several years. The achievements in terms of transfer to unsubsidised employment are not considered satisfactory, though better than in sheltered work. Similar though somewhat smaller schemes, mainly targeting persons with moderate degrees of disability, have been extended recently in the United Kingdom.

As an alternative to publicly financed employment, several countries have passed legislation which makes it compulsory for employers to have a certain percentage of disabled persons on their payrolls. Such legislation plays a significant role in Germany and Japan, and it has recently been introduced in the Netherlands.

C. A COMPARATIVE OVERVIEW OF NATIONAL PROGRAMME PRIORITIES

Labour market budgets

As indicated in the introduction to section B of this chapter, the discussion of the main programme categories will now be followed by a synthesis: the relative size of the various programme categories, the overall size of a country's labour market budget, and the number of programme participants will be reviewed and compared with that of other countries. To this end, Tables 14 to 16 show expenditure of most OECD countries for the main programme categories, the total labour market budget as a percentage of GDP, and the number of programme participants as a percentage of the labour force. Before discussing the contents of these summary and overview tables it is important to recall a number of methodological considerations which must be kept in mind when interpreting the data.

In order to classify national spending data and participants according to the present standardized classification system, a number of simplifying assumptions, definitions and concepts had to be applied. These are spelt out in the Methodological and Statistical Annex. Even with such simplifying assumptions it was often not possible to accommodate all "special cases". In addition, therefore, country-specific details with regard to the way in which certain national data have been treated can be found in the Annex.

As with all attempts to arrive at internationally comparable micro data the principal difficulty stems from differences in the institutional arrangements in individual countries. These institutional differences, in turn, reflect national traditions, priorities and customs. The present data system emphasizes the quantitative aspects and neglects the qualitative aspects of a country's labour market policy. It was already stressed in the introduction to this chapter that countries which rely more heavily on non-financial means of public action and those in which the private sector plays an important role in improving labour market outcome will appear in a less favourable light in the present data set than is actually the case. This, for instance, may well hold for countries like Japan and the United States.

Another important general consideration is that budget figures reported here measure only the ex-post amount of public resources spent on the various programmes. Thus, they do not permit a judgement as to whether the programmes themselves are effective, nor whether they are sufficient in relation to needs. If a country spends little on such programmes, this could mean either that the country has no major labour market problems to worry about; or that it gives low priority to solving these problems, or that it does not consider the available policy instruments as appropriate and effective. Conversely, high spending may reflect simply a sizeable and protracted unemployment problem – the effort could still be insufficient, ineffective or both.

In spite of these methodological difficulties, comprehensive budget data can be a useful, even if limited, guide for understanding a government's approach to labour market policy. If outlays on all the major types of labour market programmes are included, it is possible to obtain a broad picture of the priorities given by a country within the menu of available policy options. The most straightforward interpretation of the data may be to consider the relative weight countries place, or have placed, on "passive" income maintenance (unemployment compensation and early retirement) as distinct from "active" measures to help the jobless find work. Among the active measures may be distinguished, as a sub-set, those which improve labour market efficiency. Employment services, labour market training, youth measures and recruitment subsidies are examples of programmes aiming to improve the efficiency of the labour market, and hence of the economy. For other types of measures commonly referred to as "active" – such as direct job creation outside the regular labour market and certain measures for the disabled – social objectives are generally the more important consideration.

Spending profiles of OECD countries

Total public spending on labour market programmes, including income maintenance for the unemployed, varies across countries from over 5 to less than 1 per cent of GDP. In the majority of European countries and Canada it exceeds 2 per cent, whereas in Japan and the United States it amounts to just over 0.5 per cent.

Unemployment compensation is the largest single expenditure category in almost all countries. The size of this category is largely dependent on the unemployment rate. Thus in recent years, Belgium, Denmark, Ireland, the Netherlands and Spain spent the greatest

Table 14. **Public expenditure on labour market programmes as a percentage of GDP**

Programme category	Australia	Austria	Belgium	Canada	Denmark	Finland	France	Germany	Greece	Ireland	Italy	Japan
1. **Employment services and administration**	**0.10**	**0.10**	**0.18**	**0.21**	**0.09**	**0.10**	**0.12**	**0.23**	**0.07**	**0.15**	**0.08**	..
2. **Labour market training**	**0.06**	**0.09**	**0.14**	**0.27**	**0.53**	**0.26**	**0.32**	**0.30**	**0.21**	**0.58**	**0.03**	**0.03**
a) For unemployed adults and those at risk	0.05	0.09	0.13	0.22	0.25	0.26	0.28	0.23	0.02	0.40	0.03	—
b) For employed adults	0.01	—	0.01	0.05	0.28	—	0.04	0.06	0.20	0.19	—	0.03
3. **Youth measures**	**0.06**	**0.01**	**0.02**	**0.02**	**0.23**	**0.02**	**0.26**	**0.05**	**0.04**	**0.42**	**0.69**	—
a) For unemployed and disadvantaged youth	0.01	0.01	0.02	0.02	0.23	0.02	0.07	0.04	—	0.33	0.26	—
b) Apprenticeship and related general youth training	0.05	—	—	—	—	0.01	0.19	0.01	0.04	0.09	0.43	—
4. **Subsidised employment**	**0.05**	**0.04**	**0.66**	**0.02**	**0.03**	**0.50**	**0.05**	**0.20**	**0.20**	**0.30**	—	**0.11**
a) Subsidies to regular employment in the private sector	0.02	0.01	0.06	—	—	0.03	0.01	0.05	0.13	0.01	—	0.10
b) Subsidies to unemployed persons starting enterprises	—	—	0.01	—	0.03	0.03	0.03	—	0.05	0.04	—	—
c) Direct job creation (public or non-profit)	0.03	0.03	0.59	0.02	—	0.44	0.01	0.14	0.02	0.25	—	0.01
5. **Measures for the disabled**	**0.03**	**0.04**	**0.18**	—	**0.32**	**0.14**	**0.05**	**0.22**	**0.02**	—	—	**0.01**
a) Rehabilitation	0.01	0.02	0.07	—	0.18	0.04	—	0.13	0.01	—	—	0.01
b) Work	0.02	0.02	0.11	—	0.14	0.10	0.05	0.09	0.01	—	—	—
6. **Unemployment compensation**	**0.99**	**0.83**	**2.25**	**1.58**	**3.24**	**0.66**	**1.34**	**1.30**	**0.39**	**3.42**	**0.40**	**0.36**
7. **Early retirement for labour market reasons**	—	**0.14**	**0.80**	—	**1.27**	**0.56**	**0.73**	**0.02**	—	—	**0.33**	—
Total	**1.29**	**1.24**	**4.23**	**2.09**	**5.71**	**2.26**	**2.87**	**2.32**	**0.93**	**4.88**	**1.52**	**0.52**
of which:												
"Active" measures (1-5)	0.30	0.28	1.18	0.51	1.20	1.03	0.80	1.00	0.54	1.45	0.80	0.15
Income maintenance (6-7)	0.99	0.96	3.05	1.58	4.51	1.22	2.08	1.33	0.39	3.42	0.72	0.36

Source: See Annex. The figures refer to the most recent data for each country: for Luxembourg and New Zealand, 1987; otherwise 1988 or 1989 (not always the same years as in Tables 5-13).

Table 14 *(Cont'd)*. **Public expenditure on labour market programmes as a percentage of GDP**

Programme category	Luxemb.	Netherl.	N.Z.	Norway	Portugal	Spain	Sweden	Switz.	Turkey	U.K.	U.S.
1. **Employment services and administration**	**0.05**	**0.09**	**0.07**	**0.15**	**0.12**	**0.09**	**0.20**	**0.07**	**0.01**	**0.14**	**0.06**
2. **Labour market training**	**0.02**	**0.21**	**0.45**	**0.29**	**0.21**	**0.12**	**0.52**	**0.01**	**0.04**	**0.25**	**0.10**
a) For unemployed adults and those at risk	0.02	0.20	0.45	0.29	0.02	0.11	0.50	0.01	0.04	0.22	0.10
b) For employed adults	—	—	—	—	0.19	0.01	0.02	—	—	0.03	—
3. **Youth measures**	**0.10**	**0.08**	**0.01**	**0.11**	**0.11**	**0.20**	**0.06**	—	**0.06**	**0.23**	**0.03**
a) For unemployed and disadvantaged youth	0.07	0.03	—	0.11	0.02	0.18	0.06	—	—	0.01	0.03
b) Apprenticeship and related general youth training	0.02	0.05	0.01	—	0.09	0.02	—	—	0.06	0.22	—
4. **Subsidised employment**	**0.07**	**0.08**	**0.10**	**0.16**	**0.12**	**0.36**	**0.16**	—	**0.05**	**0.04**	**0.01**
a) Subsidies to regular employment in the private sector	0.07	0.04	0.08	0.02	0.05	0.02	0.02	—	—	0.04	0.01
b) Subsidies to unemployed persons starting enterprises	—	—	—	—	0.02	0.21	0.01	—	0.05	—	—
c) Direct job creation (public or non-profit)	0.01	0.04	0.03	0.14	0.05	0.12	0.14	—	—	—	0.01
5. **Measures for the disabled**	**0.28**	**0.68**	**0.02**	**0.20**	**0.05**	**0.01**	**0.74**	**0.09**	—	**0.03**	**0.04**
a) Rehabilitation	0.01	—	0.02	0.02	0.04	—	0.09	0.05	—	0.01	0.04
b) Work	0.26	0.68	—	0.18	0.01	0.01	0.65	0.04		0.02	—
6. **Unemployment compensation**	**0.31**	**2.64**	**1.06**	**1.05**	**0.31**	**2.33**	**0.60**	**0.19**	—	**0.94**	**0.38**
7. **Early retirement for labour market reasons**	**0.74**	—	—	—	—	**0.03**	**0.09**	—	—	—	—
Total	**1.57**	**3.77**	**1.71**	**1.96**	**0.91**	**3.14**	**2.38**	**0.36**	**0.16**	**1.62**	**0.62**
of which:											
"Active" measures (1-5)	0.51	1.13	0.65	0.91	0.60	0.78	1.70	0.17	0.16	0.68	0.24
Income maintenance (6-7)	1.06	2.64	1.06	1.05	0.31	2.36	0.69	0.19	—	0.94	0.38

Source: See Annex. The figures refer to the most recent data for each country: for Luxembourg and New Zealand, 1987; otherwise 1988 or 1989 (not always the same years as in Tables 5-13).

proportions of GDP on unemployment benefits – and these countries were also among those with the highest unemployment rates. In addition, of course, this expenditure depends on the rate of benefits and on the conditions of access to them; in all the five top spending countries except Spain, some benefits can be paid for unlimited periods.

Four of the same five countries also stand out as leading spenders – after Sweden – on "active" measures. The Netherlands, however, spends relatively little on any category of "active" measures other than sheltered work for the disabled. In 1988, Greece, Italy, Portugal and Sweden were the only countries where spending on income maintenance was lower than the total of "active" measures.

Belgium, Denmark, Finland, France and Luxembourg expend large resources on special *early retirement* schemes implemented in connection with labour market policies. In addition, in these countries and elsewhere, there are often provisions making the ordinary unemployment benefit schemes especially generous for older persons.

Among "active" programmes, *labour market training* for adults is the biggest spending category in several countries. In spending terms, the biggest part of labour market training is usually in the sub-category "Training for unemployed adults" – except in Denmark, Greece and Portugal, where labour market training is mostly for employed persons (see Tables 5 and 6). In the United Kingdom, as mentioned earlier, a major new programme called Employment Training was launched in 1988. In some countries the spending on adult labour market training is quite modest – both absolutely and in relation to other programmes, such as youth measures or subsidised employment. In recent years this was the case notably in Australia, Belgium, Italy, Japan, Luxembourg, Spain and Switzerland.

As discussed above, international comparison is especially difficult with regard to *youth measures*, because these must be considered in conjunction with widely differing systems of upper-secondary schools. A few facts are striking, however. Thus, Italy's labour market policies appear to be dominated by youth measures, including general as well as targeted schemes. (To some extent, Italian programmes here classified as youth measures may actually be used for adults. No separate data are available.) Other major youth programmes include those of France and the United Kingdom, which primarily provide training on the job for youth in general. Targeted programmes for disadvantaged youth are significant in Denmark, Ireland and Spain, but they also exist in many other countries.

Various forms of *subsidised employment* account for particularly large expenditures in Belgium, and substantial ones also in Finland, Germany, Greece, Ireland, New Zealand, Norway, Spain and Sweden. When this spending is large, the biggest sub-category is usually direct public-sector job creation, where costs per person tend to be high. Several countries made cuts in direct job creation after 1985; only a few of these, like New Zealand and Norway, have since replaced them by other employment subsidies on a similarly large scale. Self-employment is not the target of very large subsidy spending except in Spain – even though in terms of numbers of persons such subsidies are important in France, Ireland and the United Kingdom.

Finally, spending on special *measures for the disabled* is important mainly in northern and central European OECD countries, and particularly in the Netherlands and Sweden.

Analysis by policy objectives

The above information can be further analysed by regrouping the expenditure categories according to other policy considerations. For this regrouping the sub-categories of the seven main programme categories shown in the Methodological and Statistical Annex were used. Two distinctions of policy objectives are of special interest in terms of strategy. First, programmes aiming at economic objectives may be separated from those aiming at social objectives. Secondly, non-targeted programmes may be separated from targeted ones, or – more precisely – measures targeted on the unemployed (or people with employment problems).

The majority of "active" programmes aim, at least indirectly, to facilitate employment in regular jobs and hence to strengthen labour market adjustment and economic efficiency. Income maintenance programmes, by contrast, essentially serve social goals. The same holds, at least to some extent, for most of those "active" programmes which provide work outside the regular labour market. The latter group mainly includes the category "Direct job creation (public or non-profit)" and part of the category "Work for the disabled" – namely the sheltered work programmes[9].

Most labour market programmes are targeted on the unemployed and those at risk of becoming unemployed. However, the categories "Training for employed adults" and "Apprenticeships and related forms of general youth training" are not targeted. By separating these two categories, it is possible to isolate and tally, in an approximate manner, the total support targeted on the unemployed and other groups with employment problems.

Thus, labour market programmes can be grouped according to the nature of the main policy objective in the following way:

a) *Programmes aimed at regular jobs for the unemployed and those at risk:*
- Training for unemployed adults and those at risk;
- Measures for unemployed and disadvantaged youth;
- Subsidies to regular employment in the private sector;
- Subsidies to unemployed persons starting enterprises;
- Rehabilitation of the disabled;
- Recruitment subsidies for the disabled.

b) *Generally available programmes aimed at regular jobs:*
- Training for employed adults;
- Apprenticeships and related forms of general youth training.

c) *Programmes serving mainly social goals:*
- Unemployment compensation;
- Early retirement for labour market reasons;
- Direct job creation (public or non-profit);
- Sheltered work for the disabled.

The programme category "Employment services and administration" is not included. In order to do so, it would have been necessary to split it into three parts, which was not possible. The biggest part in most countries is connected with unemployment benefits; the rest is partly non-targeted services and partly services for the unemployed. But the entire category can also be regarded as an overhead function.

Table 15 shows the approximate distribution of public spending in 1988 (or nearest available year) on the three groups. As indicated in the introductory paragraph to this section, the figures reflect a combination of three things: the size of relevant problems in a country's labour market; *and* the political priority given to solving these problems; *and* judgements about the effectiveness of available programme tools. For example, if a government spends little on programmes assisting the jobless to find regular work, this may be because there is little unemployment, or because the government does not think labour

Table 15. **Public spending on labour market programmes[a] according to main objectives**

Per cent of GDP

Country	Helping unemployed and disadvantaged persons find regular jobs [1]	Non-targeted programmes aimed at regular jobs [2]	Socially motivated programmes for the jobless [3]	Ratio of [1] to [3] in per cent [4]
Australia	0.10	0.06	1.04	9
Austria	0.13	—	1.01	13
Belgium	0.29	0.01	3.75	8
Canada	0.24	0.05	1.60	15
Denmark	0.73	0.28	4.61	16
Finland	0.39	0.01	1.76	22
France	0.39	0.23	2.14	18
Germany	0.48	0.07	1.54	31
Greece	0.21	0.23	0.41	52
Ireland	0.78	0.28	3.67	21
Italy	0.30	0.43	0.72	41
Japan	0.11	0.03	0.36	31
Luxembourg	0.17	0.02	1.33	13
Netherlands	0.26	0.05	3.36	8
New Zealand	0.54	0.01	1.09	49
Norway	0.48	—	1.33	36
Portugal	0.15	0.28	0.36	41
Spain	0.54	0.03	2.48	22
Sweden	1.01	0.02	1.16	87
Switzerland	0.06	—	0.23	27
Turkey	0.09	0.06	—	—
United Kingdom	0.27	0.25	0.96	28
United States	0.17	—	0.38	45

a) Excluding the Public Employment Service and Administration. The figures refer to the most recent year for which data are available.
Source: See Annex.

market programmes with this goal are effective, or because the government gives low priority to this goal.

The non-targeted programmes aiming at regular jobs (column 2) are the most difficult category to compare internationally, because their functions are closely related to those of the prevailing education and training systems (see section B of Chapter IV below). The table shows, however, that Greece, Italy and Portugal devote more funds to such general programmes than to targeted measures. Other countries with sizeable non-targeted job-related programmes include Denmark, France, Ireland and the United Kingdom.

The targeted programmes (column 1) cover a few groups other than the unemployed and the disadvantaged, such as women seeking jobs traditionally held by men. Some targeted programmes are also open to a limited number of employed people when there are vacant places in public training programmes. Nevertheless the participation in these programmes is dominated by persons with employment problems. Hence it is useful to compare it with the "social" labour market programmes for the unemployed (column 3)[10]. This is done in column 4.

As can be seen, the "social treatment of unemployment" dominates in all countries except Sweden, where it is almost equal with the "economic treatment". Sometimes the two categories are of an entirely different order of magnitude. Three countries spend more than ten times as much on social programmes as they spend on job-finding programmes. These include two of those with the highest overall expenditure, Belgium and the Netherlands, as well as the moderate-spending Australia. These countries had higher unemployment than the OECD average in 1988. In other countries with higher-than-average unemployment, such as Canada, France and Spain, the ratio was in the order of 5 or 6 to 1.

Relatively low spending on social programmes compared with job-finding programmes can be found in Greece, Italy, New Zealand, Portugal, Sweden and the United States. Unemployment rates were below the OECD average in all these countries except Italy[11].

Programme participants

In 1988, over 11 million persons in the OECD area entered labour market programmes aimed at the regular job market. This corresponds to 3 per cent of the OECD labour force (Table 16). The average unemployment in the same year was 7.3 per cent. 7.7 million persons – or 2 per cent of the labour force – entered programmes aimed to help the unemployed and other targeted persons to find a job in the regular labour market. The remainder entered general youth programmes or training for employed adults.

The programme category "Training for unemployed adults and those at risk" accounts for more participants – about 3.6 million – than any other category of measures aimed at the regular job market. In several countries this category alone accounts for more than half the total number of participants in such programmes. However, some countries show a distinctively different pattern. In four countries – Denmark, Japan, Portugal and Turkey – the largest number of participants enter training programmes for employed workers. In three other countries – Australia, France and Italy – general youth schemes of the apprenticeship type are the dominating category. Finally, in Ireland and Spain, programmes for unemployed and disadvantaged youth have the highest number of entrants. In absolute numbers, the United States alone accounts for more than half of all the reported participants entering two programme categories, namely "Subsidies to regular employment including self-employment" and "Rehabilitation and recruitment subsidies for the disabled" [12].

Table 17 compares the number of participants entering labour market programmes to assist the unemployed and those at risk with the total number of unemployed. However, participant numbers represent a *flow*, or through-put, while unemployment data show a *stock*. A possible alternative would have been to use stock numbers for participants, too, where these are available. But as discussed above, this would be of limited interest from a policy perspective. It would mainly show how much unemployment is "concealed" in terms of persons being temporarily placed in programmes but who otherwise would have swelled the total number of unemployed. The assumed policy objective is to achieve placement in regular jobs as soon as possible, and not to keep people in programme activities for its own sake.

Table 16. **Participation in programmes aiming to promote permanent employment: persons starting per year as percentage of the labour force**

Country	Training for unemployed adults, etc. [1]	Training for employed adults [2]	Subsidised apprenticeships and related training [3]	Measures for unemployed and disadvantaged youth [4]	Subsidies to regular private employment including self-employment [5]	Rehabilitation and recruitment subsidies for the disabled [6]	Total	*of which:* Measures for the unemployed and disadvantaged [Cols. 1, 4, 5, 6]
Australia	0.4	—	0.8	0.2	0.6	0.1	2.1	1.3
Austria	0.9	—	—	0.3	—	0.3	1.6	1.6
Belgium	1.6	0.1	—	..	—	..	1.7	1.7
Canada	1.1	0.6	—	0.6	—	—	2.4	1.8
Denmark	1.4	5.5	—	1.8	—	1.4	10.0	4.6
Finland	1.2	—	0.1	0.4	0.5	0.6	2.9	2.8
France	2.4	1.6	2.9	1.4	0.4	—	8.6	4.1
Germany	1.5	0.8	0.5	0.4	0.2	0.7	4.0	2.7
Greece	0.1	0.5	0.3	—	1.3	—	2.2	1.4
Ireland	1.4	1.6	0.6	2.4	0.5	—	6.4	4.2
Italy	..	..	0.7[a]	..[a]	—	—	0.7	..
Japan	—	0.9	—	—	..	—	0.9	..
Netherlands	2.3	—	0.8	0.2	0.3	—	3.7	2.8
New Zealand	4.4	—	0.5	—	..	1.4	6.3	5.9
Norway	2.7	—	—	0.5	—	0.3	3.6	3.6
Portugal	0.1	0.5[a]	0.1	0.4	0.2	0.1	1.3	0.7
Spain	1.2	0.1	—	1.7	0.6	0.1	3.6	3.5
Sweden	1.7	0.5	—	0.6	0.4	0.7	3.9	3.4
Switzerland	0.3	—	—	—	—	—	0.3	0.3
Turkey	0.3	3.0	0.7	—	..	0.1	4.0	0.3
United Kingdom	1.4	0.4[a]	1.4	—	0.3	0.1	3.6	1.8
United States	1.0[b]	—	0.1	0.6	0.5	0.7	3.0	2.9
Total	1.0	0.6	0.5	0.5	0.3	0.3	3.0	2.0

The data refer to the most recent year for which they are available, i.e. in most cases 1988.

a) Several programmes are not included.

b) Excluding "Perkins Act". See Table 5.

Source: Tables 5-6, 8-10 and 12-15.

Table 17. **Participation in targeted programmes aiming at regular employment compared with the level of unemployment**

Country	Participants starting per year (thousands) [1]	Unemployed persons in 1988 (thousands) [2]	Ratio of [1] to [2] in per cent [3]
Australia	103	544	19
Austria	53	122	44
Belgium	71	424	17
Canada	240	1 046	23
Denmark	129	172	75
Finland	72	116	62
France	998	2 443	41
Germany	779	2 242	35
Greece	55	302	18
Ireland	55	220	25
Italy	200[a]	2 885	5-10
Japan	100[a]	1 550	5-10
Netherlands	170	558	31
New Zealand	92	96	96
Norway	79	69	114
Portugal	32	258	12
Spain	520	2 853	18
Sweden	154	72	214
Switzerland	9	22	40
Turkey	65	3 037	2
United Kingdom	505	2 341	22
United States	3 548[b]	6 701	53
Total	8 000	28 000	29

a) Secretariat estimate.
b) Excluding "Perkins Act". See Table 5.
Source: See Annex. The participation data refer to 1988 or nearest possible year.

On average, the annual intake of programmes to help those out of work to find regular jobs corresponds to one-quarter of the stock of total unemployment. Some countries with above-average unemployment rates (e.g. Australia, Belgium, Canada and Spain) have ratios of participation in such programmes which are lower than this OECD average. The ratio is, however, relatively high in Denmark (75 per cent) and France (41 per cent). Other countries with relatively high ratios are Austria, Finland, Germany, New Zealand, Sweden and the United States.

IV
LABOUR MARKET POLICIES RECONSIDERED

After three decades of trial and error with active manpower policies there is a considerable stock of knowledge and experience to build on. But experience has also shown that socio-economic change can make customary policies obsolete. It is therefore important to consider trends in the social and economic environment and identify, on that basis, the broad areas where policy innovation is especially important for the labour market of the 1990s. That is the purpose of this chapter. As will be seen, these policy areas go well beyond labour market policy *per se* and include, notably, social and education policies. Nevertheless this method will help identify the specific needs and challenges to which labour market policies will have to respond within a broader framework of socio-economic policy-making.

Five such broad areas of policy innovation will be discussed:

- The trend of facilitating access to work for all (the Active Society);
- The need to invest in human capital in order to respond to changing demographic and technological parameters;
- The challenge to persevere with improving the position of women in the labour market;
- The move towards a climate of innovation and entrepreneurship at local community level;
- The emphasis on raising efficiency and flexibility in the functioning of labour markets.

A. THE ACTIVE SOCIETY

When full employment was adopted as a policy goal in the early post-war period, its meaning seemed self-evident: all those who wished to find employment at prevailing wage rates were to be able to do so. By offering all "breadwinners" the opportunity to support their families, full employment ensured that mass poverty was largely eliminated. Full employment, and the economic growth associated with it, also formed the context in which the main programmes of social protection were developed and in turn greatly expanded. Health, education and old-age pension schemes were progressively extended to cover whole populations, their structure being largely, albeit not entirely, framed on the basis of the traditional family and the close links of its single (usually male) earner with regular employment. Welfare payments supported those who were unable to work or were not part of a settled family.

Throughout the 1950s and 1960s, and indeed into the early 1970s, full employment, steady economic growth and the development of social programmes proved mutually reinforcing, and in social and labour market terms achieved considerable success. The health status of populations improved, the proportion of children proceeding to higher education increased significantly, and old-age poverty was largely eliminated. Further, the systems of both unemployment compensation and general welfare support which were in place by the early 1970s were to prove very important in the latter part of the 1970s, as well as in the 1980s, in softening the social impact of high unemployment.

This environment of relatively steady growth in per-capita incomes led many OECD societies to aspire to offer all individuals the chance to escape dependency on others. However, over the last decades several developments have weakened some of the underpinnings of what had been a strong but simple, and in some areas inflexible, structure of full employment, social protection and economic growth. The initial reaction in many countries as unemployment rose was to offer income support in place of access to earned income, the hope being that the economic downturn would prove temporary, and that full employment would therefore soon be attained again. It was hoped that this support would prevent a lapse into dependence on the part of those displaced from their jobs. Unfortunately, full employment proved very difficult to restore in a number of countries, and hence the entitlement to support proved to have offered only a false independence. In many countries, inflationary pressures appeared to require higher rates of unemployment to keep them in check. Moreover, structural unemployment also appeared to have increased: the number of unfilled vacancies rose in relation to the number of unemployed.

Thus for a period, policy-makers in many countries had to live with rates of unemployment which they nonetheless regarded as unacceptable for the longer term. Perhaps even more importantly, unemployment has proved to be concentrated in particular groups (young people, older workers, the long-term unemployed), and in particular localities. Their weak links with employment-based entitlements and benefits has meant that they, together with other groups often outside the labour market such as lone parents or discouraged workers, have experienced a form of "new poverty" in which they have become isolated both economically and socially.

Accompanying these developments have been changes in family structures and indeed in employment itself, changes which have tended to weaken the previously quite direct links between employment and social protection. In some cases the changes have had positive results: the growing number of two-earner families with fewer children has of itself tended to strengthen households' links with the labour market. Only a small minority of the unemployed are now husbands in families in which no one else is employed. And where both earners have continued in full employment, households have become relatively better off. On the other hand, the search for independence has also led to greater numbers of single-person (and thereby more vulnerable) households, and the diversity of employment patterns – part-time, intermittent, temporary – has not been matched by a corresponding diversity in entitlements to social protection.

The challenge for policy-makers has been and will continue to be to reconcile these needs for social protection with the efficient and smooth functioning of labour markets. Social protection solely in the form of entitlements to income transfers, and perpetuated over a long period of time, carries the risk of discouraging re-entry into labour market activity – and thus obstructing labour market adjustment. Hence, policy has moved recently to harness income support payments to encourage rather than constrain labour market adjustment.

Income-support payments to the unemployed generally amount to less than even minimum wages in full-time work, particularly for those for whom earnings-related insurance benefits have expired. Providing training opportunities which occupy the unemployed full-time can require considerable additional expenditure – not only for direct wage costs but also for the ancillary costs of providing structured training – even if that training includes participation in productive work.

Recently, a number of initiatives have sought to escape from the constraints which these additional expenditure requirements can imply, and to move to a more sophisticated analysis of the net overall benefits from active labour market programmes. Many income-support schemes which are conditional on job search by recipients proved difficult to control adequately during the (long) periods when vacancies were considerably outnumbered by job-seekers. Thus, making income-support recipients eligible for continued support if they undertake activities to improve their readiness for the labour market can actually lead to a reduction in the total cost of the support – even if the "active" programmes are more expensive per participant than is passive support. Successfully integrating those not in employment into the labour market will always involve some displacement of those already in employment. However, unless displacement is near total, the social rate of return from reintegration should quickly repay the investment implied by the difference between the cost of income support and that of more active measures.

A number of countries have recently introduced initiatives which reflect such thinking. In those countries where unemployment benefits were previously available to teenagers on the same basis as to adults – for example Australia, New Zealand and Sweden – income support for teenagers is now conditional on participation in some form of training and/or part-time employment. In the United Kingdom unemployment benefit is no longer available to those under 18 because of a government guarantee to provide the 16 and 17 year-olds with some form of training or employment. Unemployment benefit systems for adults are being revised to emphasize active measures in Australia, Canada and Sweden. The recent welfare reform in the United States has attempted to eliminate those features of the income-support system which discouraged labour force participation by lone parents. In France a new minimum income scheme (*revenu minimum d'insertion*) is designed to link in with measures for reintegration into society.

Such approaches are requiring a diversion of resources from merely maintaining the incomes of those who are unemployed, disabled or lone parents to finding ways in which they can participate in economic life. In such reform programmes, the goal is to find other guided forms of training and employment which will preserve income-security entitlements while encouraging actual labour force participation. If this involves an extension of part-time employment, it is generally not in the context of "sharing out" existing full-time posts, but rather to encourage higher labour force participation.

B. THE QUALITY OF LABOUR SUPPLY

Education and the economy

Labour supply has two main dimensions: the number of people willing to work and what they can do. The latter dimension, the quality of labour supply or "human capital", is likely to become more important in a situation where the quantity of young people entering the labour market is shrinking. One challenge for public policies, therefore, will be to compensate for a declining supply of youth by mobilising other sources of potential supply. In addition to raising the labour market participation of various adult groups, one important objective would be to upgrade the skill level of the labour force. This would also be in line with the increasing awareness that human capital in technology-driven economies is becoming a decisive factor in contributing to economic performance.

The concern about an emerging "skill gap" results not from future demographic and technological trends alone. In several countries it is rooted in the past and present maladjustment of the education and training system to the world of work, or the inadequate size of that system relative to the demands of a modern economy. It is feared that in these countries a more or less general discrepancy is emerging between qualifications which come on-stream through education and training, and the human capital inputs required for economic growth. Such a situation is felt to be particularly serious by countries which are less advanced in terms of industrial development or by those which, on the contrary, have been industrial leaders in the past. For them a prolonged period of under-investment or unproductive investment in human capital could easily lead to lower real wage growth (and ensuing inflationary pressures) and lower returns on physical capital (and ensuing protectionist pressures). However, it is true for all OECD countries that with growing global economic interdependence ahead, national concerns about possible skill gaps and international competitiveness must figure high on the policy agenda.

Against this background, an Intergovernmental Conference on Education and the Economy in a Changing Society was held in 1988 at OECD [OECD (1989*a*)]. The Conference highlighted the interaction between education and the economy at three levels: initial education, further education and higher education. It stressed the need to involve all actors in the process of change and reform: public and private education institutions, education and labour market authorities, representatives of workers and employers. The Conference noted that forecasting skill needs was notoriously unreliable. This puts a premium on flexibility. To this end a key objective must be "to impart to all young people a broad base of transferable skills", and this responsibility was seen as resting on both schools and employers. For adults, "the private sector in particular must assume primary responsibility for the provision of training and retraining opportunities". Another basic idea which emerged at the Conference was the desirability of developing training markets in which many different styles and contents of training would be available. Governments in such markets were seen as participating as deliverers of training but also as playing a co-ordinating and standard-setting role.

It is worth noting that the Conference did not draw strict lines between the responsibilities of different actors. Nor did it distinguish between the responsibilities of different branches of government, either institutionally (i.e. between government departments) or functionally (i.e. between policy areas). It recognised that both government and the private sector have responsibilities for youth as well as adults – although the role ascribed to employers was relatively more important in relation to adults. In accordance with this attitude of "non-interference" with national practices, it was also left open to what extent governments should provide or finance vocational education and training or to what extent they should merely regulate these activities. This implies that the implementation of the general principles pronounced by the Conference will differ from country to country, given the variety of institutional frameworks. In particular, the policy options will depend on national education institutions as well as existing traditions of enterprise-based training.

The Conference was above all a general demonstration of intent by OECD countries to create closer links between their education systems and economies than in the past. This raises the question of whether, and in what terms, training and retraining as an instrument of labour market policy will still have a role to play once this overall adjustment between education and the economy, with a view to upgrading the skill level of the labour force, has been achieved. The following two sub-sections discuss, from a labour market perspective, policy issues arising from current education systems and enterprise-based training in OECD countries; in the last sub-section an attempt will be made to answer this question.

The structure of general education

It is possible, as indicated in Chapter III and documented in Table 18, to distinguish three groups of OECD countries according to the basic structure of the education they provide for young people[13]. In Japan and North America, the great majority of young people go through high school and many continue in post-secondary education as well. Most vocational skills are acquired after age 18, mainly in enterprises, although there are also schools and colleges with vocational programmes.

Two types of potential labour market problems may be identified as associated, at least in part, with these education systems. First, the opportunities open to poor performers and high-school drop-outs are often very limited because further education and vocational

Table 18. **Education enrolment of 17-year-olds as percentage of total age cohort**
School year 1986-87

Country	Full-time education	Part-time education	Total
Australia[a]	40	10	50
Austria[b]	35	43	78
Belgium	82	5	86
Canada	79	—	79
Denmark	..	..	75
Finland	83	..	..
France	69	10	80
Germany	51	48	99
Greece[b]	59	..	..
Ireland[b]	65	..	..
Japan[a]	89	2	91
New Zealand[b]	37	1	39
Netherlands	78	—	78
Norway	74	2	76
Spain[a]	53	..	..
Sweden	83	..	..
Switzerland	27	56	83
Turkey[a]	32	..	..
United Kingdom	33	16[c]	49
United States	89	—	89
Yugoslavia	66	—	66

a) Excluding third level education.
b) 1985-86.
c) Including the Youth Training Scheme.
Source: *Education in OECD countries 1986-87*, OECD, Paris, 1989.

training, where available, tend to require a high-school diploma. This accentuates the risk of exclusion, especially among minorities and in particular areas such as inner cities in the United States. Secondly, the content of vocational training is generally less uniform and transparent, and hence certified skills are less easily portable in these countries than in countries with more institutionalised vocational training and certification systems (see below). *A priori*, low transparency of skills will reduce efficiency in the allocation of specialised labour. In some vocational areas, specialised labour markets may not develop at all without a widely-accepted certification system. This may in turn discourage workers from investing time and money in acquiring the skills concerned. However, if mobility between enterprises is low – as it often is in Japan – then employers will have more incentive to invest their money in training and will develop internal labour markets. In North America, by contrast, mobility between firms may often be too great for employers to invest in training. The combination of high mobility and low portability of job-related skills may thus lead to insufficient investment in training, because incentives may then be too weak for both employers and workers.

In Austria, Germany and Switzerland, formal training for vocational skills is highly structured and plays a greater quantitative role than in other countries. About half of each cohort of 16-18 year-olds follow "dual" apprenticeship programmes as part of upper-secondary education. Most of the others attend academic or technical upper-secondary schools. But the numbers of those who go on to post-secondary study are modest by international standards.

The dual apprenticeship systems combine vocational training, provided by employers, with part-time general education provided in schools. Adult training is also common in these countries and often designed to be compatible with apprenticeships. Taken as a whole, this environment offers attractive career pathways for large parts of the population – including most of those whose school performance is not outstanding. As a result, youth unemployment is moderate compared with the situation in other countries. But the system displays some rigidity. In most localities, vocational and academic tracks are separate already in lower-secondary school, and specialisation is relatively great throughout the system. Crossovers are common but they often cost time, raising the average age that students reach before completing education. The development of training for new needs is possible only if established procedures are followed. The agreement of all parties involved is necessary – although particular efforts are undertaken to minimise possible delays.

In some other European countries as well as Australia and New Zealand the labour market problems caused – directly or indirectly – by deficiencies in upper-secondary education are often considerable. The basic problem is that there are too few attractive training opportunities for young people who have below-average educational achievements. This poses an immediate difficulty for many who are looking for their first jobs. An equally unfortunate consequence is that many will later find themselves ill-prepared for adult training.

The proportion of young people receiving an academic secondary education preparing them for university is typically less than one-half in these countries. What happens to the remainder of each youth cohort differs between countries. Finland, France, the Netherlands and Sweden train large numbers in a variety of vocational and technical education courses. These are mostly provided in schools, but sometimes on the job. They have occasionally proved very successful; but often they suffer from a bad image which reduces the market value of the diplomas awarded. In most Mediterranean countries, the United Kingdom, Australia and New Zealand there are still relatively large numbers of young people entering the labour market without upper-secondary educational qualifications or with only rudimentary ones. Technical and vocational upper-secondary schools exist in all these countries, too, as do apprenticeships. But they cater for too small proportions of the youth cohorts. Labour market programmes fill part of the gap, but on the whole these too are insufficient in relation to the size of the youth employment problems.

The absence in some countries of well-established vocational training systems for youth also adds to the institutional obstacles facing labour market authorities when they try to provide training for adults. Training standards and curricula may have to be developed from scratch. In principle this can be done, but the training may still fail to win market acceptance, especially if it does not conform to established hiring practices. This is probably one reason why programmes for training unemployed adults have generally been of limited importance in the last-mentioned group of countries. But several governments, including notably that of the United Kingdom, have announced their determination to overcome these difficulties by promoting new forms of co-operation with employers.

Enterprise-based training

The Conference mentioned above has stressed the prime responsibility of employers for providing job-related training. Such training is increasingly important in the context of the new technologies where skill requirements evolve rapidly and *pari passu* with the introduction of new processes and products. Since skills are one form of capital, training should be subject to profitability calculations in the same way as investments in tangible capital. The parallel with tangible capital is often used to underline the long-term value of skills for the enterprise; but it also helps to understand the complexity of the training decision and the difficulty of forecasting training needs. It follows that governments cannot know what and how much training is needed in enterprises any more than they can know what sort and how much machinery should be purchased.

Nonetheless, OECD governments have undertaken a variety of policy measures designed to influence corporate training decisions. Although the overall impact of these measures may be seen as marginal, hardly any government has renounced them altogether. As discussed briefly in Chapter III, the relevant policies can include both subsidies and a spectrum of regulatory controls. The subsidies may be general or more or less narrowly targeted. Regulations may focus either on quantitative variables such as training expenditure – as in France – or the number of persons involved. Alternatively, governments may only regulate the content of curricula, examinations, or other institutional features such as co-operation between enterprises. Germany provides an example of this more qualitative approach.

Unfortunately, the existing information about training in enterprises is very scarce. As described in Chapter III, a few countries including France, Germany and Ireland have set up institutional frameworks requiring some amount of reporting by firms about their training efforts. Elsewhere, special surveys have been carried out. However, the quantitative data thus available are difficult to interpret. Contents, intensity and work relevance of this training are likely to vary significantly between establishments and countries. Moreover, a significant amount of training is in the form of experienced workers helping less experienced workers to get acquainted with equipment and work functions. This form of training, which in terms of human capital and productivity is probably most worthwhile for enterprises, will not be caught in any statistics.

Special caution is also needed regarding cost estimates. The largest part of training costs – where they are reported – usually consists of the wages paid to the trainees (or the continuation of their normal pay). It is, however, difficult to judge to what extent trainee wages ought to be regarded as a training cost. That depends, among other things, on whether or not the trainees produce anything of value during the training period. To the extent that this is the case, the net costs are smaller than the actual wage bill. Similarly, a significant part of reported non-wage training costs typically represent the use of buildings and equipment and the wages of fellow-employees giving instruction. Inclusion of these items at their full nominal value may imply a gross over-representation of actual training costs. The opportunity costs of on-the-job training are much lower if buildings, equipment and staff are under-utilised or simultaneously used for other productive activities. Indeed, one major rationale for pursuing vocational training in enterprises is precisely that the opportunity costs are relatively low.

For these reasons, it is important to stress that data on company-based training – including reported numbers of trainees and training hours – are not only difficult to come by but must also be interpreted with extreme caution if they are to be used for policy purposes.

Thus, while it is beyond doubt that adequate levels of enterprise-based skill formation is an important goal for public policy, it is extremely difficult or impossible to control its most crucial elements. Governments will have to content themselves with creating a favourable environment for in-firm training. Improvements in this environment are probably best achieved by long-term measures which affect the whole range of institutions in each country's education system and its labour market. If the behaviour of private employers cannot be fundamentally altered by direct controls or financial incentives, an alternative approach for governments may be to seek indirect effects by setting examples within the public sector. If these examples are good, they may also have an impact on training standards in the private sector and in the entire labour market. Indeed, it is likely that both public vocational schools and training centres for the unemployed will occasionally be able to play such a pace-setting role.

Another possible strategy for governments is actively to promote co-operation within industry and between industry and education providers. This usually involves some financial support, which may be relatively modest or limited in time. In Germany, for instance, a considerable expansion of industry-wide and co-operative training centres has been achieved by such means. Industries can, however, hardly be expected to make co-operative efforts unless there is sufficient consensus within each industry about what type of training is needed. The potential role of government is thus largely to serve as a catalyst, not fundamentally to change the economics of training.

Functions of labour market training

All labour market training and retraining programmes can be said to have one thing in common: they must supply the needs of groups that are not (or not sufficiently) catered for by the systems of general education, vocational education and training or by company-based training. From this perspective it is not surprising that labour market training sometimes appears to lack a clear focus. It has to respond to a wide and heterogeneous set of shortfalls in the supply of skills, shortfalls which prevent the labour market from clearing. Moreover, when there is a conflict between addressing acute, short-term needs and projected long-term "skill gaps", labour market training generally has to give priority to the former. It must first help those out of work and relieve the skill shortages that are reflected by current job vacancies as they are signalled to the Public Employment Service. The rationale for pursuing training and retraining programmes in connection with PES services is that this information can be brought to bear. Potential synergies are available in the form of more efficient job placement and more job-relevant training. However, in responding to short-term skill mismatches, labour market training and retraining programmes have to be compatible with the long-term policy orientations which a country has chosen in terms of up-skilling and human resource development – hence the need for close and permanent co-operation between labour market authorities, education authorities and the private sector.

The targeting of labour market training will have to vary over time and between countries. It is, however, likely that unemployed persons will remain the most important target group for the foreseeable future. Given current labour market trends, training for the unemployed needs to be further developed and more strictly oriented toward skills in short supply. There is a more general reason why governments have to finance or to provide training for the unemployed. If vocational training were left exclusively to private employers, adverse externalities for the labour market at large would arise. Most labour markets have a tendency to become segmented, with enterprise-based training offered mainly to a "core" labour force enjoying relatively high degrees of employment security. Therefore, unless government assumes special responsibility for training the unemployed, a significant minority will risk becoming locked into a "peripheral" workforce, characterised by unskilled temporary jobs and recurrent spells of unemployment.

Labour market training has to be provided in different ways depending on the existing institutions in each country. In countries where there is a well-established vocational training system for young people (school- or enterprise-based), training for unemployed adults should harmonize with the essential elements of this system. If possible, curricula and examinations should correspond to those already known and accepted in the labour market. It is often necessary, however, to develop new and shorter training modules which can be more readily combined according to individual needs. In countries or industries without a well-established vocational training system, the difficulties of designing effective training programmes for the unemployed are often considerable. It is essential that the difficulties in the normal vocational education and training area be addressed, something which takes time and requires consensus-building within the industry concerned about training contents, training standards and financing arrangements. Even if labour market authorities are not normally responsible for setting training standards, in these latter countries they may face the need to play a leading role in this respect resulting from their experience with designing training programmes for the unemployed.

It is generally useful for labour market training to be implemented in a decentralised manner, with the participation of employers, local union representatives and local education providers. There are, however, examples of excessive decentralisation. The parties involved may pursue different objectives. Thus it is important that labour market authorities exert leadership to ensure that the training serves its purpose. As a rule, it should be the responsibility of the Public Employment Service to decide both which trainees are to be accepted and what training is to be offered.

Some training programmes have been fraught with problems caused by poor relations between labour market authorities and training providers. Often, labour market authorities tend to regard established training institutions as insufficiently flexible, so that they turn to employers for training for unemployed people. Enterprise-based training for the unemployed has, on the whole, shown good results, but training in educational establishments should not be abandoned. On the contrary, there are indications that employers, too, are increasingly turning to specialised institutions for their training needs. Thus a greater involvement of employers may not eliminate the need for training centres – but no doubt it will place them in a new situation. It is likely that they will be put under increasing pressure to respond to employers' needs, in particular if the employers provide financial support.

Policy issues are somewhat different with regard to the youth training schemes which labour market authorities run in some countries. Some of these programmes are now seen almost as a "normal" step for youth entering the labour market: the trainees often come directly from school and do not have to prove that they cannot find a job. The programmes concerned may therefore in future become gradually more integrated into the ordinary education system. This, in combination with demographic trends, may gradually reduce the need for labour market authorities to address the particular problems facing school-leavers.

C. THE POSITION OF WOMEN IN THE LABOUR MARKET

The access of women to the labour market and their advancement in the economy warrants particular attention. Their growing participation in the labour force is one of the basic secular trends at work in virtually all OECD countries. The trend is not new, but it is certainly the most significant long-term structural change in labour supply. This has immediate implications for the operation of the labour market and for labour market policies, and its effects are also felt in all other parts of society. While this process is steady and long-term, it is far from smooth. Institutional and behavioural inertias, as well as countervailing forces, have to be coped with, both by the individuals concerned and by public policy. OECD governments have clearly stated their position in the 1980 Declaration on Policies for the Employment of Women: "Men and women, as equal members of the society, should have equal opportunities for paid employment, independently of the rate of economic growth and conditions in the labour market" [OECD (1980)]. Hence OECD governments are committed to facilitating the integration of women into the labour market and to ensuring the equality of treatment and opportunity.

This requires a close monitoring of progress (or otherwise) of the position of women in the labour market as well as a regular examination and, if necessary, a readjustment or basic reform or strengthening of policies to maintain progress. A recent statistical analysis of female labour market trends by the Secretariat has shown the following results.

The last twenty years have seen a particularly rapid growth of female activity rates in virtually every OECD Member country except those of Southern Europe. The greatest increases have been in the Nordic countries, where female participation rates now approach those of men. The patterns of activity by age seem to be associated with a progression from societies where labour force participation ceases upon marriage, to others where it is suspended during the years of child-rearing, and finally to those where it is not possible to detect any change in overall female participation rates as women pass through the different stages of family-building.

The rise in participation rates has been accompanied by two other major changes in female activity over the life-cycle: a fall in the proportion of women responsible for the care of young children and a rise in the number of women carrying the "double burden" of professional and child-rearing responsibilities (many of whom work part-time). As a consequence, a higher proportion of the female workforce is building up long periods of continuous labour market experience, and hence is in a position to establish and maintain higher-level skills.

In most countries women have higher measured unemployment rates than do men. Despite the fact that women can now be found in virtually every occupation, they are still concentrated in just a few and are particularly under-represented in senior positions. Indices of the dissimilarity of male and female employment across the major industrial and occupational groups have declined only slowly, if at all, over the past thirty years. Part of the reason for this is that the rapid growth of employment in the service sector has attracted large numbers of women into a relatively small number of occupations. There appears to be no uniform tendency for the dissimilarity between employment patterns of young men and women to be any less pronounced than for their elders.

Turning to the different types of employment, part-time work is done mainly by women – though most women work full-time. Adult women are not much more likely to work on a temporary basis than are adult men, at least in the countries of the European Community. However, the type of temporary work done tends to differ, as do the reasons for undertaking temporary work. The self-employed are mainly men, but in several countries the female share of self-employment has increased.

Average female earnings remain considerably lower than average male earnings. However, for Australia and most European countries, statistics of hourly earnings of manual workers in manufacturing reveal a widespread and often substantial increase in relative female earnings since the 1960s. In a number of countries, over half of the total differential between men and women has been eliminated. Although change often levelled off in the 1980s, statistics covering all workers show a considerable increase in female earnings in Canada and the United States.

To sum up: over the past twenty years, women have made considerable progress in entering the labour market. Yet there is a long way to go before they could be said to have achieved equality with men, either in terms of the type of jobs they do or the remuneration they receive. Against this background a recent OECD evaluation panel on Equal Employment Opportunity Policies and Programmes has attempted to identify the main barriers which still exist to the full and equal participation of women in the labour market. The panel has summarised these barriers as follows.

Differential earnings: The fact that women's average earnings are still markedly less than men's reduces women's economic incentive to work and their capacity to achieve economic independence through economic activity.

Occupational and industrial segregation: The different labour markets operate with a varied but identifiable degree of occupational and industrial segregation which prevent or inhibit women from participating in all segments and sectors of the workforce. This means that the majority of women are concentrated in a narrow range of occupations, the lower end of occupations, in low-status industries and in occupations with limited career paths or promotional or training opportunities.

Family responsibilities: Many women still have the burden of a "double day", as they also carry the major responsibility for family and domestic duties. This occurs because of societal expectations about the different roles of women and men in the family, and the assumption that men are the primary wage-earners. These responsibilities restrict the time and effort women can devote to paid employment, and affect the expectations that employers have about women employees in general. Attitudes and behaviour by employers based on assumptions about women's family responsibilities often effectively limit or deny women access to jobs, training or promotion.

Child care: The availability of safe, affordable child care is a major determinant of the employment expectations and opportunities for women with dependent children.

Social attitudes: In some communities, the expectations of the role women will perform is a severe restriction on the nature and type of employment they can undertake. Some societies operate on an explicit assumption that women as primary care-providers will not seriously enter the job market, and so will not provide a permanent workforce. These expectations are reflected in the type and curriculum of school and post-school education women undertake and the occupations they enter. Attitudes can prevent women from competing equally with men for jobs, and in particular for senior positions even if they have the necessary skills, experience and qualifications.

"Non-traditional" jobs: Even when women are trained in jobs where the majority of employees are men, they are faced with barriers in finding a position, in maintaining it, and in gaining access to benefits such as promotion and further training opportunities. Women entering a totally male work environment frequently have to confront overt and covert resistance from male workers, often expressed through sexual harassment. There are few external support systems or mechanisms to assist them in maintaining their employment and dealing with issues such as sexual harassment.

Education: The different educational experiences of women and men affect the employment expectations and opportunities of both groups. Therefore, it may not be a deliberate choice for a girl to go down a particular path, as societal expectations may have already influenced the parameters around her choice. Consequently, access to new technology training may not be readily available to girls, as they do not have the prerequisite skills or proper advice and counselling, and so they are denied access to the "new" jobs, and the status and earning potential which goes with those jobs.

Protective legislation: In some countries, there are some legal restrictions on the type of work women can undertake and the hours they can work. Underground mining and jobs involving lead manufacture may be denied to women, as may jobs where heavy weights have to be lifted. Work after midnight or overtime beyond a certain number of hours per week may be prohibited.

Mandatory retirement age: In some countries, an earlier mandatory retirement age for women acts to limit their long-term employment and opportunities for promotion, as employers know women will be with the organisation for a shorter period than equivalent male workers. Mandatory early retirements also have the effect of reducing retirement incomes for older women.

Interrupted working life: The majority of women have some breaks in their working lives for child-birth and -rearing but seldom for acquiring additional skills. Employer expectations are frequently based on a male work pattern, that is, an uninterrupted work span. Broken work patterns can mean that women lose their work skills and are unable to compete with men of an equivalent age, especially in areas where new technology or work practices have been introduced.

Security: Many women work in marginal jobs, and are especially vulnerable to redundancy during economic downturns. Also, where women are viewed as being a secondary, and non-vital, part of the labour market their situations are less secure than men's. In some countries, where women work a low number of hours per week or have a non-continuous work history, they are below the threshold for contributions to social security or insufficiently covered and therefore do not qualify for benefits when in need.

Part-time work: Denial of many benefits provided by an employer, including promotion, sick leave and holiday pay, can arise when a person is employed part-time. These restrictions can mean the part-time workers are continually denied benefits and their service in that part of the workforce is not recognised if they move into full-time work. As noted above, the vast majority of part-time workers are women.

In order to overcome these barriers, OECD Member governments pursue a variety of policies. In the field of policies on equal pay, comparable worth and equal employment opportunity, there appears to be a shift from traditional "equal rights" concepts, outlawing direct discrimination, to "positive action" or "affirmative action" programmes aimed at modifying employment systems. Such policies have been specially designed to combat the disparate impact of traditional employment practices on women's access to jobs and promotion opportunities.

Empirical evidence on the effectiveness of equal pay and equal employment opportunity policies is still scarce and hard to interpret, particularly because of the general increase in female labour force participation and the difficulty of isolating appropriate control groups to permit rigorous empirical investigation. As regards pay differentials, the effects of recent equal pay policies seem particularly evident in Australia and the United Kingdom. When looking at the impact of affirmative action policies on occupational segregation, several studies have found positive effects of legislation and special administrative programmes, particularly in the United States.

For the future, the evaluation panel referred to above has pronounced itself in favour of a more ambitious and active policy stance. The panel considered that voluntary action was generally inadequate, because of the extent of the inequality between women and men in the labour market. Without active and effective intervention, the labour market will continue to reproduce this inequality, so that there is a clear need for positive or affirmative action programmes. Regardless of whether these programmes are based on incentives or mandatory requirements, they should prevent discrimination at the point of selection for posts.

In order to be effective, these programmes must be ambitious both within their reach (i.e. beyond pilot programmes) and in their scope and use of resources. They should cover the initial education of youth, child care, public service infrastructures and public information programmes and all the factors that support or provide flexibility to women in the labour market.

D. LOCAL DEVELOPMENT

One manifestation of structural (as distinct from cyclical) change is the uneven pattern of industrial development. Employment has been declining in the traditional heavy industries in which large firms predominate. In the field of service sector employment there has been an increase in employment in small firms, but much less in some types of large service sector enterprises and especially in public services. One of the consequences of this development has been the uneven regional distribution of unemployment and its persistence over time observed in many countries [OECD (1989*b*)].

The response to this combination of factors has focused attention on the urgency of operating labour market policies to meet the needs of highly differentiated local labour markets. One attempt to examine the requirements for such an approach was the creation of an OECD evaluation panel on Decentralised Delivery of Manpower Measures, which showed that all thirteen countries taking part in the panel had in fact adopted some degree of decentralisation. The general conclusion drawn from this work was that whilst decentralisation presented a challenge, bringing new elements and indeed complications into the decision-making process, it also held out promise because it widened the pool of experience and initiative.

A more general response has been to involve actors other than merely the labour market authorities and to stimulate the creation of new enterprises at local level. These efforts have relied on harnessing local talents, expertise and resources rather than a more traditional emphasis on across-the-board financial incentives to expand employment or efforts to attract industry from outside the local community. It was an approach which first gained prominence in France and Italy at the beginning of the 1980s, and spread rapidly to other parts of Europe and regions further afield. Awareness of this development led the OECD to start its own Co-operative Action Programme on Local Initiatives for Employment Creation (ILE) in 1982. At their meeting in 1986, the Ministers of Labour and Social Affairs of the OECD countries agreed that such initiatives were an essential part of a new approach to increasing the job intensity of growth.

In the ILE Programme the new concept has been further developed with regard to local development, innovation and entrepreneurship. This approach is characterised by the following objectives and arguments.

Local actors and partnerships: Effective efforts to develop local employment build on the capacity of local actors: people working in business, banks, universities, trade unions, or active in voluntary organisations and political life. Often the most important role that government can play is to bring these people together in an interactive and informal way with a view to encouraging project-based partnerships.

Assessment of local potential: Local development policies are most successful when time is taken to analyse the local economies before taking action. New programmes or agencies should not be created without an understanding of the area's real strengths and weaknesses. A careful assessment – or "strategic audit" – can provide the information needed in order to develop appropriate action.

Decentralisation: Local employment and economic development initiatives work best when they are comprehensive but decentralised. This constitutes a significant advantage over programmes designed and implemented at regional or national level. Healthy local development is multifaceted and diversified. It is important, therefore, that local initiatives are not narrowly conceived and do not deal with only one aspect of the problem.

Intellectual infrastructure: In modern economies, rapid growth tends to cluster in areas which have universities, research laboratories and sophisticated networks for investors and entrepreneurs who turn innovative ideas into new products and processes. Areas therefore need to look at how they can improve their intellectual infrastructures. They can improve their higher education system, fund research institutions, and create programmes which bring academic and business researchers together to carry out applied research with commercial potential. However, regional or national co-ordination is required in order to ensure that areas do not compete excessively against each other or duplicate effort.

Local educational initiatives: The critical importance of education to employment growth has led governments to devote considerable energy to educational reforms including a greater awareness of, and new approaches to, the role of local educational establishments in shaping young people's attitudes to self-employment and enterprise. Those who wish to create a business need the skills to run one. Training initiatives of local enterprises and sandwich courses are important for those already in the labour market or else seeking to re-enter it, and thus for strengthening the competitive edge of the local economy.

New patterns of private investment: The principal objective must be to encourage additional private investment, not to substitute public for private investment. It is important that local communities try to influence the way in which private funds are invested in order to enhance economic growth and job opportunities at the local level. To change private investment patterns, local government can act as a catalyst in the creation of new private-sector institutions, it can act as a broker to the private sector by bringing different parties together, it can leverage private-sector action with public investments, and it can create public/private partnerships.

Improved access to risk capital: One essential element of an entrepreneurial climate is the supply of risk capital. Many governments, including local and regional authorities, have set up public or quasi-public venture capital institutions and loan funds; some have invested parts of their pension funds in small business loans or equity. Other approaches to encourage more venturesome investment behaviour and the formation of new private institutions would be the provision of loan guarantees and the creation of seed funds, business support centres and industrial development corporations.

Industrial modernisation: If regions and areas are to be competitive, innovation cannot be limited to new enterprises. Mature companies must also modernise their technologies and adopt production methods that allow them to make adjustments to rapidly changing markets. To encourage this process, local authorities can establish so-called "industrial extension systems" in which consultants help firms to choose the automated equipment they need to remain competitive, train their workforce to use it and reorganise production techniques so as to improve productivity within each company.

Information and orientation: Local employment and economic development programmes need feedback mechanisms on new products and processes in order to be effective. Any programme designed to nurture economic growth must be able to anticipate market trends, and public/private partnerships run by people with wide experience of responding to market change are well placed to create such mechanisms.

Improving the entrepreneurial climate: Many areas that might have appeared well endowed with major universities and attractive qualities of life have not experienced significant growth. They seem to lack the intangible elements that encourage people to start new companies and to pursue new ventures and hence create new employment. Local partnerships for job creation and economic development should therefore respond with business assistance centres, small business incubators, financing programmes for new small businesses and other efforts to stimulate entrepreneurship.

E. LABOUR MARKET EFFICIENCY

Internal and external labour market flexibility

The way in which labour is allocated and reallocated among enterprises, i.e. the functioning of the external labour market, is the primary concern of public policy. But the efficacy of this policy will be influenced by the way in which labour is allocated and reallocated within enterprises. Labour markets, whether internal or external ones, will clear through quantity adjustments or price (i.e. wage) adjustments or – in the normal and most effective case – both. Hence, policies to improve the functioning of labour markets should preferably include all the major dimensions of flexibility: external and internal adjustments as well as adjustments of quantities and prices. The last dimension, wage adjustments, is relevant in two respects: (i) the movements of the overall level of nominal wages relative to the overall rate of inflation; (ii) the movement of wages for particular types of labour (age groups, skills, industries, regions) relative to other types of labour. Earlier work by the Secretariat [OECD (1986*b*)] has shown that both forms of wage adjustment have some effect on employment, i.e. countries or industries which have experienced a swift downward adjustment of wages have also experienced a better employment performance than others.

Several countries have adopted policies towards wage differentials, for instance by tolerating the erosion of minimum wage floors (i.e. by not adjusting the nominal minima to price increases). Other countries have responded to high youth unemployment in the early 1980s by seeking lower entry-level wages relative to average wages. Resisting pay claims in the public sector and containing trade union power or increasing competition in product markets have been other strategies. The rationale for increasing labour market flexibility through labour market policies is different: the emphasis here is not on price but on quantity adjustments. The main targets for policy are the redeployment of workers within firms (internal flexibility) and the mobility of workers between firms (external flexibility).

While the influence of public policy on the organisation and functioning of internal labour markets may be limited, it is by no means negligible, as is demonstrated by job security legislation introduced, mostly in Europe, in the 1960s and 1970s. Providing workers with job security and firms with job stability has become mutually advantageous for both sides of industry. There is an extensive literature on this point which cannot be reported here. In essence the argument is as follows. One factor tying workers more closely to firms has been the growing importance of on-the-job training. To some extent, such training ties the worker to the firm during boom periods because some elements of the acquired skills are firm-specific and hence cannot be sold in the open market. Conversely, employers keep workers during slack periods in order to reap the benefits of their training investment over the longest possible time. However, only skilled workers will benefit. Unskilled workers, on the contrary, tend to be hired and fired frequently and thus used as a buffer between a relatively protected core labour force and cyclical fluctuations of demand. There is a danger, therefore, that the "internalisation" of labour markets will be accompanied by a segmentation of the labour force between those in stable, well-paid career jobs and those in short-term, casual jobs with poor career prospects.

This concern with a growing segmentation of the labour market led trade unions in the 1960s and 1970s to negotiate agreements which would increase employment protection generally. A first wave of agreements improved individual employment protection, especially from unjust dismissals. Procedures and valid grounds for dismissal were defined, as well as the extended periods of notice, severance pay and supplementary income maintenance provisions in cases of dismissal. In a second wave of agreements additional provisions were introduced for workers facing collective redundancies and for older workers affected by rationalisation of production methods. Many of these negotiated provisions were subsequently incorporated into comprehensive national legislation, thus covering all sectors (including, for instance, small enterprises) and all workers (including peripheral workers) who did not benefit from internal labour market practices.

Europe was most affected by these waves of mandatory or negotiated job security provisions. The welfare state still shaped thinking in Europe in the 1970s, well after macroeconomic performance had begun to deteriorate following the first oil-price shock. Eventually, however – for some disturbingly late – the new economic situation brought about a change of attitude. The "crisis of the welfare state" was accompanied by a growing concern with a host of rules and regulations which had grown up over the years or were the product of outdated institutional settings, especially in the area of industrial relations. Although many of these provisions were motivated by social concerns or were genuinely necessary in their time, they were now felt to hinder the rapid and smooth reallocation of resources and hence to harm economic performance.

Forceful counter-arguments to deregulation emerged as well, expressed most clearly in "neo-corporatist" and "neo-industrialist" schools of thought [Streeck (1989)]. The first school is in favour of strong and assertive trade unions which can play a positive role – based on "negotiated" social solutions – in the process of adjustment to structural change. The second school of thought is rooted in the current debate on the new technologies and their potential to overturn Taylorist mass production methods and work organisation. It argues for diversified production, participative management, up-skilling and high wage strategies. Both schools are opposed to the creation of a highly competitive environment in the labour market. These arguments go well beyond an academic debate. Indeed, the current political negotiations between the EEC member countries on a Social Charter for the post-1992 Single European Market bear witness to these fundamental concerns. Whatever the detailed outcome of these negotiations, it is fairly certain that Europe will maintain a strong social dimension in its market economy and that this will predominantly affect the labour market [Emerson (1988)].

In modern labour markets there are normally two sources of flexibility: functional (internal) flexibility allows workers who enjoy job security and company-based training to accept technological change, to be redeployed and to adjust to new work assignments; numerical (external) flexibility permits enterprises to adjust the size of their total workforce to fluctuations in product demand. While individual enterprises – subject to production constraints – may prefer one of these strategies, it is seldom possible to rely on one approach alone. The same is true for the economy at large. In the future, therefore, a reasonable balance will have to be found between internal and external flexibility. The challenge for public policy will be to preserve the advantages of internal labour markets, but at the same time to prevent access to these markets from being limited to certain workers and completely foreclosed to others – hence to ensure that a certain degree of external flexibility is maintained.

New technologies and internal labour markets

The characteristics of internal labour markets and the way they function are likely to change quite substantially under the influence of new technologies, especially information technologies. These technologies are as pervasive and cost-effective as the earlier revolutionary developments of the steam engine or electricity supply. Yet aggregate productivity growth has slowed down throughout the OECD area over the past decade. One of the possible explanations for this "productivity paradox" is that the social environment has not been sufficiently adaptive to, and supportive of, a rapid diffusion and exploitation of these technologies. In particular, the reluctance of firms to change their work organisation, labour relations, decision-making structures and management styles means that the spread of information technologies is currently slower than it could be, or is not achieving the full potential productivity gains. Pressure from international competition is bound to speed up the process, and the appropriate social environment within enterprises could play an important role in determining future technology leaders and laggards.

The full exploitation of the new technologies implies a shift away from the "Taylorist" model of production typical of the previous phase of industrialisation, which was concentrated (although not exclusively) in manufacturing and was based on fragmented work tasks, long production runs and hierarchical control. By contrast, the new technologies permit the frequent reprogramming of existing equipment, short production runs and hence a prompt responsiveness to changing market needs. Workers, however, must be able to master a greater number of more varied skills since work tasks can no longer be fragmented and small-batch production does not allow for the same degree of trial and error as was possible in the case of mass production. Also required are behavioural skills and attitudes relating to initiative, judgement and communication, particularly in service industries, where growth continues to be more rapid than in manufacturing sectors.

Enterprise-based skill training will be more effective if workers are motivated to constantly extend and enlarge their skills on the job, which means that it is important to provide appropriate incentives. It has been argued [OECD (1988*b*)] that payment linked to general competence rather than to immediate performance and productivity could have this effect, as workers would be rewarded according to their potential and not simply for their current output. This potential could be increased by adding new skills, but also by motivation, versatility and other positive work attitudes. Under such a system, both firms and individuals might be better prepared to cope with technological change and to work out mutually acceptable solutions for redefining jobs and redeploying human resources within the enterprise.

Similar benefits would accrue from overcoming rigid and narrow job classifications and job demarcations, features that are particularly serious and difficult to change in countries with craft unions, although significant reforms have already started under the pressure of international competition and technological change. Given the uncertainties about the direction of future change, there is now a premium on multi-skilling and the blurring of occupational boundaries. In large Japanese firms, for instance, the classification of workers by occupations is virtually unknown, and this accounts for much of the internal flexibility with which Japanese businesses have been able to adapt to change.

In addition to competence-based pay systems and blurred job boundaries, a third key element in the future development of internal labour markets could consist of new methods and styles of management. With the demise of fragmented work tasks, hierarchical control will become more difficult. It may have to be replaced by two-way information flows and participative management. Workers' participation in decision-making and the various models of co-determination have, of course, been the subject of a long-standing and unresolved debate which is likely to be revived as a result of pressures from the new technologies and the associated need to modify work organisation. According to a recent OECD report on new technologies in the 1990s, prepared by a group of independent experts [OECD (1988*b*)], the competitive strength of enterprises, industries and national economies will depend on these innovative developments.

Should governments leave the organisation of internal labour markets completely to private initiative? To the extent that they are themselves major employers, this option is by definition excluded. But governments also have a wider responsibility. As already mentioned, it is in the public interest to maintain a reasonable balance between external and internal flexibility. The moves towards the "internalisation" of labour markets in connection with new technologies are likely to tie the workers even more closely to their firms and to cut them off from the open labour market. Likewise, enterprises may become so dependent on their own workforce that they no longer try to compare the qualifications and skills they might obtain on the open market with what they already have. This could easily lead to a situation in which external market transactions and market pricing of particular skills would disappear.

For these reasons some minimum level of regulation or provision negotiated between the social partners should ensure flexibility in both internal and external labour markets. In particular this will be indispensable when old job boundaries are removed and broader job classifications are introduced. A public vocational training system, for instance, will mean maintaining a certain number of well-defined job categories for which curricula and diplomas will have to be specified and followed. Similarly, if pay scales become increasingly based on all-round competence, some collectively agreed and defined standards of competence will be needed so that the system is clear to all participants in the labour market and so that wages can act as market signals in the economy at large. This would imply, for instance, that workers have a right to have the details of their range of skills and work history regularly certified by their current employers so that they can make them available to prospective new employers.

Labour market policies to improve external flexibility

While labour market regulations will need to be adjusted to the evolving economic and technological environment, they can hardly replace traditional tools of labour market policy such as training, placement and mobility measures. These measures improve the efficiency of the external labour market by speeding up adjustments to structural change. At the same time they have a strong equity element in that they aim to equalise access to job opportunities for all workers, including new entrants to the labour market.

Present prospects for the 1990s do not suggest that the emphasis of labour market policies will shift back to job-creation measures. This holds in particular for public sector programmes, whereas the use of incremental employment subsidies targeted on specific workers and circumstances may continue to play a certain role. Even less likely is the re-emergence of policies to reduce labour supply (early retirement, return migration, shorter working hours, etc.) which have been pursued by some countries in the 1970s and early 1980s with a view to balancing the available number of jobs with the number of job-seekers. Given the relative decline of young age cohorts and the concern to create an Active Society, labour market policies will rather aim to raise labour force participation over a wide range of the working-age population.

Rising levels of labour force participation have become typical in highly-industrialised countries, especially as more women enter the labour market. However, when labour markets became depressed in the 1970s and early 1980s participation rates for older men and young people of both sexes fell. This may well have been an involuntary phenomenon and the desire to become economically active appears to be an unabated secular trend in OECD countries. The policy task, therefore, reaches well beyond finding jobs for those currently unemployed.

The absorption of potential labour supply will not be automatic. The view commonly held in the past that "a strong tide will lift all boats" would be a dangerous attitude to rely on. More complex production methods and forms of work organisation, the interplay of physical and intangible capital, rising standards of living and aspirations of workers have all contributed to raising adjustment and transition costs. Furthermore, the legacy of a prolonged period of labour market slack in Europe and the long-standing exclusion from the labour force of disadvantaged groups in North America, strongly suggest that structural mismatch and inertia have been built up.

The best guarantee for achieving the maximum amount of absorption is to ensure that labour markets function as effectively as possible and that public policy assists those who are at risk of falling behind. This again will place a premium on traditional labour market measures which achieve equity and efficiency objectives simultaneously, i.e. placement, training and mobility schemes. However, these measures will have to be adapted to the needs of the 1990s and will have to be better co-ordinated with related policy areas than in the past, notably with education and social policies.

Labour adjustment policies for adults are likely to become key elements in efforts to enhance labour market efficiency in the 1990s. The need to take action in this area is the counterpart of the decline in youth labour supply described above. An economy undergoing structural change can adjust its labour resources smoothly and effectively by channelling young people entering the labour market into the growth sectors. Sectors in decline, conversely, can be made to shrink through natural attrition. Hence, provided the speed of structural change is not too rapid relative to economic growth, a country with a labour force growing younger (rather than one that is ageing) will be able to reallocate its labour resources without forcing adult workers to change jobs and activities. The risk of labour displacement and dislocations will therefore be minimal. By contrast, this risk will rise when the labour force is ageing, which is the outlook for the 1990s and beyond. Moreover, the prospects of rapid technological change, as well as shifts in trade (Single European Market, new generation of newly-industrialised economies), will increase the need for reallocation and hence put severe adjustment pressures upon the adult labour force. Thanks to the baby boom effect, there will be a large cohort of adult workers in the labour force who are still relatively young during the 1990s, and their adjustment potential can be expected to remain strong, a factor which public policy should exploit.

The problem of displaced workers has already come to the fore in several countries. It is most severe where older workers and communities with single-industry economies are affected. There is considerable variety in how countries address the problem. Only a few resort to labour market policies explicitly designed to assist displaced workers. More common are legislative or collective bargaining provisions (advanced notice, social plans, reconversion leave), as well as *ad hoc* initiatives taken by the PES (for instance, special placement offices created on the premises of major plants which are shutting down). It appears that in the past many older workers displaced by structural change have simply withdrawn from the labour market and become dependent on income transfers. Over the coming decade a stronger policy emphasis will be required in this area and new programmes will have to be devised.

The most effective approach would be to develop strategies to assist workers before they are actually laid off and are simply threatened by structural change or, even better, to act preventively by enhancing their ability to cope with change. Two main policy directions can be envisaged:

i) increase the possibilities of redefining jobs, up-skilling and redeployment within the firm; and

ii) further education and training of the adult labour force.

The first has already been discussed in the framework of internal labour markets; the second will to a great extent be the responsibility of education authorities and has been discussed in Chapter IV, section B. Yet it would be illusory to assume that the need for structural change could be met by preventive strategies alone. Since the direction of change is largely unpredictable, labour market disequilibria for specific jobs and skills are bound to occur, so that the authorities must have in place a battery of remedial labour market programmes as well as robust and flexible techniques to implement them.

V
POLICY ORIENTATIONS FOR THE FUTURE

The changing thrust of labour market policies

The priorities for labour market policies and the socio-economic environment within which they operate have undergone significant changes since 1976, when the OECD Council adopted the Recommendation on a General Employment and Manpower Policy. The need to accommodate structural change has put a premium on policies which improve the functioning and flexibility of the labour market. A properly functioning labour market will ensure that labour is continuously and swiftly directed – within the firm and the economy as a whole – to its most productive and rewarding use. This will permit more rapid structural change and hence economic growth than a situation characterised by institutional rigidities, a plethora of regulations and a climate of resistance to change. Deregulation and programmes aimed at increasing labour market efficiency have therefore come to the fore, and labour market policies have to be viewed as a key element in an overall strategy to improve the functioning of product and factor markets. The emphasis on a wide range of micro policies is now regarded as crucial for macro-economic performance – more so than in the past, when such a result was thought to be essentially dependent on the pursuit of appropriate macro policies.

In most countries, however, it has proved to be extremely difficult to deregulate labour markets. On reflection, this is not surprising. The allocation of labour resources has to meet efficiency criteria but, unlike most other markets, the allocative function of the labour market is strongly conditioned by the prevailing societal consensus on social standards and norms of equity. Some of these standards are common to virtually all highly-industrialised countries (for instance, equal pay for equal work, prohibition of child labour, equal job opportunities through public schooling), others are more country-specific (for instance, minimum wage floors, seniority rights, paid maternity leave). Any deregulation which touches on these consensus-based provisions has to be built on a new consensus to dismantle them – something notoriously difficult to achieve. For these reasons progress in deregulating the labour market has been slow even in those countries that have made major efforts in this direction, the exception being a few major reforms of the industrial relations systems in a small number of countries.

In Chapter III recent attempts to change rules and regulations were documented in three areas: wage-setting machinery, employment and redundancy legislation, and working-time arrangements. These show that considerable efforts have been made and that the modifications are by no means negligible if one regards them as changes to the "rules of the game" rather than simply as cut-backs in the regulatory framework. Other examples discussed in Chapter IV show that additional regulations would be required to improve labour market efficiency, for instance training and work certificates in order to ensure the transferability of skills and mobility. Therefore, the experience so far would suggest that there must be a permanent concern that the regulatory framework is compatible with the evolving socio-economic situation in each individual country. In other words, it is the quality rather than the quantity of rules and regulations that is relevant for labour market performance.

The detailed review of labour market programmes in Chapter III reveals that in most countries there has been a substantial shift towards training measures. It has been increasingly recognised that labour market training has to be tailored both to the needs of individuals or groups with specific employment problems and to rapidly-changing market needs. Labour market training has to be co-ordinated with vocational education and training provided by private industry and the formal education system. There has been less reliance over the last decade on temporary job-creation measures in the public sector. Some emphasis was placed instead on indirect job-creation via enterprise creation and on the involvement of various actors – notably non-governmental bodies – in local employment initiatives. Job-seekers were encouraged to start their own businesses by various means, including access to lump-sum unemployment compensation entitlements. New initiatives have been undertaken to strengthen job search, job motivation and job readiness, particularly in conjunction with the fight against long-term unemployment. Several countries have reformed their Public Employment Service with the aim of improving its effectiveness in facilitating labour adjustments – often targeted on specific industrial restructuring projects.

These developments clearly point in the direction of greater market efficiency, but with the important proviso that individuals are given help in adapting to change. They are neither "feather bedded" (as an extreme form of welfare state thinking would imply) nor are groups with undue adjustment burdens left completely to their own devices, as would happen if there were radical deregulation. Nevertheless, the analysis of expenditure data shows that, in most countries, more could be done within current budget lines to improve labour market efficiency by shifting priorities from income maintenance to "active" measures, and from a "social treatment of unemployment" to a more economic one.

The new context of the 1990s

Despite persistently high levels of unemployment in many OECD countries, the 1990s could well become a period of sustained growth of output and employment. The rapid diffusion of new technologies and their effective economic and social exploitation is likely to generate new economic opportunities, new forms of work organisation and more varied combinations of work and leisure time [OECD (1988*b*)]. There is also reason to be confident about the continuing internationalisation of the world economy, not least due to governmental efforts to further liberalise trade and to contain protectionist pressures. The transition from planned to market economies in many countries of Eastern Europe is likely to boost world trade and economic growth.

These positive developments on the demand side will occur at a time when demographic shifts will reduce the growth of the working-age population in most OECD countries. Both trends taken together could, in theory, provide a unique opportunity to lower persistently high rates of unemployment and to reintegrate disadvantaged groups into the labour market, particularly those with long records of unemployment and/or labour force detachment. There is a reasonable chance that not only the long-awaited goal of full employment may come within reach in many OECD countries, but that "activity for all" who strive for gainful employment may become an attainable reality.

However, such promising results will not come about automatically, for several reasons:

- The legacy of a prolonged period of labour market slack in Europe and labour force detachment of disadvantaged groups in North America suggest that structural mismatch and inertia have built up;
- Under-investment in human capital resulting from low profitability of private industry during the recession has led to a skill gap in some countries. This will become increasingly obvious as the new technologies spread rapidly and an information society comes into being;
- The slowdown in the growth of the working-age population will first lead to a smaller number of young people entering the labour market. Countries that so far have relied on a "vintage" approach to renew their human capital stock, i.e. on young people being equipped with new skills and familiar with new technologies, may therefore encounter difficulties in the future;
- A network of welfare provisions has shielded most people in the highly-industrialised countries from deprivation and extreme hardship during the world recession. This positive outcome may have an unintended side-effect, however, which is becoming increasingly apparent during the period of recovery: many groups have become completely dependent on income transfers, and the incentives to seek to enter (or re-enter) the labour market may not be sufficient.

These are not the only risks and uncertainties involved. It is difficult to assess the future labour market effects of the slower growth and rapid ageing of the populations of OECD countries alongside the explosive growth of the world population. The same holds true for the labour market implications of the Single European Market which the EEC countries have pledged to create by 1993. Even more uncertain are the ramifications of the new geopolitical realities created by the reform process in the Eastern European countries. These developments will have wide-ranging repercussions on OECD economies and societies, and will thereby affect the labour market indirectly and possibly directly through international migration.

In the past, international migration has often been a more or less spontaneous response to wealth differentials and differentials in available labour or skill resources. The world recession, however, triggered off by the oil-price shocks has sharply reduced job opportunities, hindering the successful integration of migrants in the host countries. Restrictive migration policies have therefore been adopted, in particular by the European OECD countries. Yet migration flows have not entirely stopped. Family reunion, illegal migration, skilled migrants, populations of the same ethnic origin as the host country, refugees and asylum-seekers continue to play a significant role. Global changes point to more, rather than less, human migration flows in the future.

There are limits to the capacity of restrictions and coercion to control migration flows effectively. More needs to be done by way of positive policies, and in the first place by mobilising domestic human resources in the receiving countries. Such a labour supply strategy, which will be further outlined below, would include the integration and up-skilling of migrants residing in the country and the rapid labour market integration of new legal entrants. The more successful such a labour supply policy, the smaller will be the demand pressures from inside the country. In order to contain the supply pressures from outside, the most effective means would be to help the potential emigration countries with their economic development, notably by investing in these countries (i.e. bringing the jobs to where the workers are). Finally, there should be more rather than less room for the migration of highly skilled persons, in particular those who wish to gather international experience before continuing their careers at home. This would make it possible to reap the benefits of international migration in both sending and receiving countries.

A socially responsible labour supply policy

From both the shifting emphasis of labour market policies since the 1970s and the new challenges taking shape in the 1990s a clear message seems to emerge for future policy-making. Labour supply should be strengthened in all its dimensions: overall size, quality, flexibility – both inside and outside the firm – and at national and local level. A socially responsible labour supply policy would reduce the risk that a non-inflationary expansion of output might be hindered by sluggish labour market adjustment, that disadvantaged groups might not benefit from increased job opportunities, and that migration might become a substitute for adjustments of the production system instead of an opportunity for the mutual enrichment of sending and receiving countries. There is a wide spectrum over which the functioning of labour markets could be improved and labour supply trends enhanced: from mobilising the full potential of female labour force participation, reintegrating the long-term unemployed and recipients of transfer incomes into the labour market, to raising the quality of labour supply by upgrading the skill level of the workforce, and to creating a climate of innovation and entrepreneurship especially at local level.

These objectives would all form part of the Active Society approach as outlined in Chapter IV, section A, but they would go well beyond the scope of what can be achieved by traditional labour market policies and programmes. They require a co-ordinated effort comprising education policies, social policies, equal opportunity policies, as well as regional and local development policies. Moreover, micro policies in these various areas will be successful only within a framework of sound macro-economic policies and expanding employment.

Active policies to strengthen labour supply will induce more people to seek gainful employment. These policies will be more successful in a climate of expanding job opportunities. Conversely, labour supply policies will further improve growth prospects. The challenge, therefore, is to create a virtuous circle between economic growth and labour market integration.

Co-operation must embrace not only various government departments and other relevant official agencies but also the private sector, including business and trade unions. The need for such policy co-ordination has always existed, but there is now a new dimension in that major breakthroughs are occurring, notably in educational and social policy. Furthermore, the Active Society approach provides an underpinning to the various policy areas concerned. The better integration of different policy areas would also permit greater cost-effectiveness and transparency. This would improve the possibility for redistributing tasks in the labour market, social and education areas between the public and the private sector.

A more integrated policy approach

In the *social policy* area, the general aim should be – as expressed by the 1988 meeting of the Manpower and Social Affairs Committee at Ministerial level – to create a political and social consensus to reform and integrate employment and social protection policies so that they foster economic opportunity and activity for all individuals. In this new, wider perception other groups have to be served by labour market (rather than social) policies, for instance those in poverty, those who have become over-dependent on income transfers and those who have become alienated from society and live in isolation.

The growing awareness of *education* authorities and the business community that there is an urgent need to co-operate, notably in the area of adult education, has been clearly demonstrated at the 1988 Intergovernmental Conference on Education and the Economy in a Changing Society [OECD (1989*a*)]. From a labour market perspective (see Chapter IV, section B above), this attitude is to be warmly welcomed: the more these new developments succeed in preparing young people for the world of work and adults for coping with change, the easier it will be for a complementary labour market policy – and labour market training as one of its principal instruments – to take remedial action for those who may still encounter employment problems.

In the area of *equal opportunity policy* for women, the main direction of necessary action inside and outside governments was spelled out in the Declaration of the 1980 High Level Conference on the Employment of Women [OECD (1980)]. With the gradual improvement of employment conditions, the situation of women in the labour market could, in principle, be markedly improved in the years to come. This will require an undiminished commitment by governments and the social partners to persist with their efforts both in pursuing equal opportunity policies *per se* and in dealing with the broader aspects of policies for women in such areas as education, tax and social security policies. Particular attention should be given to flexible working arrangements and an appropriate infrastructure (child care, training facilities, public transport, shopping facilities, etc.) which is still missing or insufficient in many countries and which adversely affects education, labour market and career prospects for women. To assist in this process, the setting up of a high-level group of experts has been proposed by the Working Party on the Role of Women in the Economy and endorsed by the OECD Council.

The ILE Programme of the OECD bears witness to the strong desire of Member countries to create a climate of *innovation and entrepreneurship at local level.* The reconsideration and reassessment of physical and human resources available at local level and the encouragement of individual and collective initiatives to make use of these resources has proved to be a viable approach for developing and revitalising local economies. From a labour market perspective this movement responds to the overall objective of strengthening labour supply trends by integrating or reintegrating people affected by regional and local imbalances or structural shifts in economic activity.

Policy priorities for the labour market

There are limits to which the contents and use of national policy instruments can or should be agreed upon at international level. However, the growing economic interdependence of OECD countries calls for a joint search for viable solutions and a coherent policy framework. What is at stake is not so much that inappropriate labour market policies of one country might harm another country. But not adhering to a common policy thrust could imply that individual countries might fall behind in the stiffer competitive environment of the world economy. Hence the rationale for international co-operation in the area of labour market policy.

Future labour market policies will not necessarily require completely new policy instruments to be designed and introduced, but rather a reform and a shift of emphasis. The concept of a socially responsible labour supply policy would suggest action in three priority areas.

Improving the quality of labour supply

With technological change ahead and insufficient national effort in some countries in the past, the need for human resource development is compelling. The urgency is further heightened because in quantitative terms the potential growth of labour supply will slow down in the years to come, as fewer young people enter the labour market. One option to offset the shrinking quantity is to raise the quality of the labour supply. This implies better and more co-ordinated initial education and skill training for young people, as well as – and most importantly – new and increased efforts to upgrade the skill level of adults.

The burden of action will fall on the general education system, together with the vocational education and training providers and, in particular, private industry. The precise role of labour market training will differ between Member countries according to the institutional arrangements of the formal education and training system and the scope and contents of company-based training. As was argued in Chapter IV, section B, the primary focus of labour market training must be on achieving a short-term match between skills in demand and skills on offer. This implies that labour market training will primarily be short-term and remedial in nature, and it will mainly have to cater for the unemployed and those at risk of becoming unemployed. In addition, however, given that labour market authorities are in close contact with the market in their day-to-day operations – in particular in dealing with market failures in the form of unemployment – they should also serve as a catalyst for, and participate in, decision-making on long-term human resource development, be it in the area of formal education and training or enterprise-based training.

Improving labour market flexibility

Deregulating the labour market in order to increase its flexibility and efficiency has become a policy objective in many countries. However, experience shows that it is extremely difficult to dismantle labour market regulations. Moreover, there has been a growing realisation that too much emphasis on making the external labour market more flexible could mean a reduction in the flexibility and efficiency of internal labour markets. Some argue, for instance, that job security of workers is the *quid pro quo* for their favourable attitude towards technological change.

It is important, therefore, to maintain a balance and to ensure complementarity between internal and external flexibility (see Chapter IV, section E). Public policy should steer a middle course between two risks:

i) that too high a degree of external labour market flexibility adversely affects the up-skilling, job redesign and redeployment of workers within the enterprise; and

ii) that too strong an "internalisation" of the labour market impinges on the economy-wide reallocation of labour and segments the labour force between those with secure, career jobs and those with casual, dead-end jobs.

Whether there is a case for government intervention will depend on the particular circumstances, the size of the structural shifts which have to be accommodated, prevailing management styles and prerogatives, industrial relation systems and cultural factors. However, governments have the ultimate responsibility of creating a climate in which innovation and change take place and that this occurs in a socially acceptable way.

The propensity of workers to change employment in order to seek better jobs and career opportunities elsewhere will be enhanced by wage structures which reflect as accurately and promptly as possible the changing skill shortages and surpluses in the economy. It has to be recognised, however, that wage differentials are embedded in a net of rules and norms which, in turn, are often anchored in historical developments and strong social perceptions. The role of wage differentials as market signals and incentives will therefore be limited, and adjustments in differentials will in many countries be too slow in relation to the speed of structural change and the ensuing need to reallocate labour. Hence the importance of labour adjustment policies. Nevertheless, over the longer run it is important that wage differentials do eventually reflect changing market conditions in order to prevent misallocations and thus to reduce the potential growths of output, incomes and jobs.

Facilitating access to jobs and adjustment to structural change

Strengthening the expansion and responsiveness of labour supply will require that everybody be given the means to compete successfully in the labour market. The ultimate goal of such a strategy must be to offer all potential workers access to employment. Even under conditions of continued steady growth this is still a formidable challenge. Many countries have had to come to terms with a serious and protracted problem of long-term unemployment or labour force detachment of disadvantaged groups, such as ethnic minorities, inner-city youth or displaced older workers with obsolete skills. These groups tend to remain unresponsive to demand pressures if their employability is not enhanced through public policy action.

In spite of recent efforts to improve the balance, most OECD countries still spend more on passive than active measures, and more on the "social treatment of unemployment" than on programmes which raise the competitive strength of the unemployed in the open labour market. (This has been documented in Chapter III.) A major shift of priorities would be needed if the challenge to absorb all potential workers were to be met. This shift would not only imply a lower share of spending on income maintenance but also a switch away from direct job-creation programmes in the public sector (which in most countries has already taken place). Programmes to reduce labour supply, notably schemes that result in a general reduction of retirement ages, do not fit into this framework either. Conversely, the new framework suggests a special emphasis on placement, mobility and training measures.

The brokerage function of the Public Employment Service calls for a wide market coverage, including catering for job-seekers who are currently employed and for companies in which vacancies may emerge only in the future. A strong PES with a certain institutional and financial independence – however not necessarily in a monopoly position – would be best suited to meet this objective. It would also be well placed to provide labour market information on which other activities – such as training and local development strategies – might build. Finally, a strong PES would ensure the effective implementation of labour market programmes since experience has shown that in order to be successful, these programmes need a solid institutional infrastructure. Too often they are implemented hastily in order to respond to a crisis situation or to short-term political needs. The work of the OECD evaluation panels has shown that the *ad hoc* nature and weak institutional support for programmes, rather than their design, was often responsible for poor results.

New policy initiatives will be required to strengthen job search, job motivation and job readiness. Several countries have already developed new approaches of this kind as part of their efforts to fight long-term unemployment (see Chapter III, section B). In future, a more generalised strategy of facilitating labour market access will have to be available for various groups now catered for by social policies. Their dependency on income support alone will have to be replaced by a combination of active reintegration policies, positive incentives to search for work and a safety net in the form of minimum income security. A rising activity rate for the working-age population could contribute to the long-term macro-social requirement of improving the tax base for the financing of social security.

Youth labour supply will fall. Increased adjustment pressures will therefore fall on adults. The most effective way of meeting this new challenge will be by preventive action through the regular up-skilling and multi-skilling of workers. This will be the task of enterprises (possibly subsidised by public authorities in certain circumstances) and the formal education institutions. The Public Employment Service should provide new forms of counselling services for adults with a view to strengthening their capacity to cope with structural change and to improve their career development. However, preventive action of this nature will never be sufficient to foreclose all possibilities of displacement and obsolescence. Hence, remedial labour-market programmes to assist adult workers affected, or threatened, by structural change will demand greater policy efforts in the years to come.

Notes and references

1. They urged the OECD, therefore, to organise "a meeting of independent experts of world-wide standing with the task of giving thought, in a scientific context, to the definition of active policies for achieving a better balance between the supply of and demand for employment, for a given level of activity" [OECD (1976)]. The meeting was held in 1977 ("Stoleru Conference") and the proceedings published [OECD (1977*b*) Vol. I and (1979) Vol. II].
2. The latter developments will be further documented in this report.
3. Shares vary between 1/10 and 1/6 for Austria, Canada, the Netherlands and Switzerland; 1/4 for France; 1/3 for Australia, Germany and the United Kingdom; and 2/3 for Sweden.
4. In Finland, labour force surveys in 1985 included questions about how persons starting jobs received the information that led to employment. According to this source, 16 per cent of the jobs were taken up as a result of public employment services. In 42 per cent of the cases information was given directly by the employers, while in the remaining cases it was provided by newspapers (22 per cent) or friends and relatives (20 per cent) [Finland (1987)].
5. The results for Germany and Ireland have been reported in an OECD evaluation panel on Occupational Training and Retraining Programmes for Specific Target Groups; for Finland, the Government's account to Parliament concerning measures for the application of the Employment Act, Helsinki 1987; for Sweden, see AMS Research Unit, Report No. 1989:9.
6. In certain contexts, the definition of "youth programme" has been taken to be very wide, sometimes covering all measures in favour of persons younger than 25 or even 30 years. Within the European Community, for instance, the rules governing the Social Fund have encouraged member governments to stipulate 25 years as the upper age limit for a large number of programmes.
7. In some countries these policy developments may have increased the enrolment rates for the 17-year-olds above the 1986/87 levels quoted in Table 18.
8. In the Spanish system, a deduction is allowed from either employer or employee income declared for taxation. In 1988 the deduction was 500 000 pesetas or about four months' average wages per additional worker employed.
9. As shown in the Methodological and Statistical Annex, most of the category "Work for the disabled" consists of sheltered work. These measures generally have little or no impact on the regular labour market. But in some countries, especially Finland, Norway and Sweden, part of the category consists of subsidies for disabled persons hired in regular jobs. This difference of programme content has been considered as far as the data permit.
10. Some of the socially-motivated labour market programmes, such as early retirement for labour market reasons, may concern persons who have not previously been registered as unemployed. These persons are nonetheless out of work, and with few exceptions their situation is a direct consequence of unemployment.
11. If available, standardized unemployment rates, as published by the OECD, have been used.
12. Column 6 in Table 16 includes, for a few countries, the recruitment subsidies listed as part of the category "Work for the disabled".
13. A comparative review of education and training in OECD countries, seen from an economic perspective, was provided in *Structural Adjustment and Economic Performance*, Chapter 1 [OECD (1987)].

Bibliography

AMS (1989), Follow-up study on course participants who terminated labour market training in 1988 [in Swedish], Report No. 1989:9 by the Research Unit, Stockholm.

BUECHTEMANN, C. (1989), "More jobs through less employment protection? Evidence for West Germany", *LABOUR: Review of Labour Economics and Industrial Relations*, Vol. 3, Winter 1989/1990, Berlin.

CEREQ (Centre d'études et de recherches sur les qualifications) (1989), *Cereq Bref*, No. 45, Paris, July.

DOBELL, A.R. (1981), "Social policy-making in the 1980s: elements and issues". In: *The Welfare State in Crisis*, OECD, Paris, pp. 227-239.

DYMOND, W.R. (1989), "Manpower Measures: Synthesis of the Main Findings of the Evaluation Programme", OECD, Paris (document for general distribution).

EMERSON, M. (1988), "Regulation or deregulation of the labour market", *European Economic Review*, No. 32, pp. 775-817, North Holland.

FINLAND (1987), "Government's account to Parliament regarding measures for application of the 1986 law on employment", Helsinki.

HAVEMAN, Robert H. and SAKS, Daniel, H. (1985), "Transatlantic lessons for employment and training policy", *Industrial Relations*, Vol. 24, No. 1, Winter, pp. 20-36.

OECD (1962), *Policies for Economic Growth*, Paris.

OECD (1964), "Recommendation of the Council on Manpower Policy as a Means for the Promotion of Economic Growth", Paris.

OECD (1970*a*), *Inflation. The Present Problem*, Paris.

OECD (1970*b*), *Trends and Innovations in Manpower Policy, 1967-69*, Paris.

OECD (1972), *Adult Training as an Instrument of Active Manpower Policy*, Paris.

OECD (1976), *Ministers of Labour and the Problems of Employment*, Vol. I, p. 74, Paris.

OECD (1977*a*), *Towards Full Employment and Price Stability*. A report to the OECD by a group of independent experts under the chairmanship of Paul McCracken. Paris.

OECD (1977*b*), *Structural Determinants of Employment and Unemployment*, Vol. I, Paris.

OECD (1979), *Structural Determinants of Employment and Unemployment*, Vol. II, Paris.

OECD (1980), *Women and Employment: Policies for Equal Opportunities*, Paris.

OECD (1981), *The Welfare State in Crisis*, Paris.

OECD (1985), *Employment Growth and Structural Change*, Paris.

OECD (1986*a*), "Labour Market Flexibility". Report by a high-level group of experts to the Secretary-General under the chairmanship of Ralf Dahrendorf. Paris.

OECD (1986*b*), *Flexibility in the Labour Market. The Current Debate*, Paris.

OECD (1987), *Structural Adjustment and Economic Performance*, Chapter 1, Paris.

OECD (1988*a*), *Measures to Assist the Long-Term Unemployed. Recent Experience in Some OECD Countries,* Paris.

OECD (1988*b*), *New Technologies in the 1990s: A Socio-economic Strategy*, Paris.

OECD (1989*a*), *Education and the Economy in a Changing Society*, Paris.

OECD (1989*b*) *Employment Outlook*, Chapter 3, Paris.

OECD (1989*c*), "Self-employment schemes for the unemployed", *ILE Notebooks*, No. 10, Paris.

OECD (1989*d*), *Japan at Work: Markets, Management and Flexibility*, Paris.

STREECK, W. (1989), "On the social and political conditions of diversified quality production", paper presented at the Conference on "No Way to Full Employment?", WZB, Berlin, July.

ULMAN, L. (1974), "The uses and limits of manpower policy", *The Public Interest,* No. 34. Winter.

OECD (1988a) *Measures to Assist the Long-Term Unemployed. Recent Experience in Some OECD Countries*, Paris.

OECD (1988b) *New Technologies in the 1990s: A Socio-economic Strategy*, Paris.

OECD (1989a) *Education and the Economy in a Changing Society*, Paris.

OECD (1989b) *Employment Outlook*, Chapter 2, Paris.

OECD (1989c) "Self-employment schemes for the unemployed", *ILE Notebooks* No. 10, Paris.

OECD (1989d) *Japan at Work: Markets, Management and Flexibility*, Paris.

STREECK, W. (1989), "On the social and political conditions of diversified quality production", paper presented at the conference on "No Way to Full Employment?", WZB, Berlin, July.

ULMAN, L. (1974), "The uses and limits of manpower policy", *The Public Interest*, No. 34, Winter.

Annex

A. METHODOLOGICAL NOTES ON PUBLIC EXPENDITURE DATA AND PROGRAMME CATEGORIES

In principle, the objective is to include all public outlays for relevant programmes, regardless of which branch or level of government is involved. Hence, relevant activities of ministries or agencies other than those normally in charge of labour market policy have, as far as possible, been taken into account. The same holds also for government expenditure at state, regional and local level. However, because labour market policies are in most countries primarily a responsibility of central government, such expenditure at decentralised level does not normally seem to play a major role – even in countries with a federal administrative structure.

When central labour market authorities partially finance activities managed by other public or private bodies, the latter's own financial contributions have in most cases not been considered as part of the national labour market budget. The underlying reason for this practice is that the partial contributions by the central authorities are usually the essential "labour market policy" element of the activities concerned, whereas the subsidiary bodies are more likely to have different reasons for paying their contributions, for example local development or environmental preservation. This accounting rule, however, is simply a statistical convention, which may in different countries do more or less justice to the actual situation. In a few cases, however, it was regarded as appropriate to include matching contributions by regional authorities. This has been indicated in the footnotes to the country tables.

No distinction has been made between expenses of national Treasuries and those of other public or quasi-public sources of finance, such as unemployment insurance systems funded by compulsory employer and/or employee contributions. Income foregone through reductions in taxes and social security contributions has also been included as expenditure. However, only those schemes targeted on particular labour market groups would fall into this category; across-the-board cuts in employer taxes, for example, would not. Similarly, a general cut in payroll tax to raise the demand for labour would be viewed as a macro-economic, rather than a labour market policy measure.

Further difficulties arise when a categorisation of different policy measures suitable for international comparison is to be achieved. The principal challenge in this respect is to find for all countries a common denominator which is both rational in terms of policy concepts and practical in terms of data availability. It has not proved possible, for example, to develop categories defined uniformly on a functional basis; thus, two of the main categories – youth programmes and measures for the disabled – relate to target groups, while the others relate to functions.

In a first step, seven main programme categories have been established. Expenditure data in this classification have already been published in the *Employment Outlook*. In a second step, a number of sub-categories within the seven main categories have been established. Obviously, the difficulties of grouping national data on a comparative basis are higher the narrower the categories chosen. Additional caution is needed therefore in making international comparisons for particular sub-categories.

The categories and sub-categories have been defined as follows.

1. Public employment services and administration

The following services are included: placement, counselling and vocational guidance; job-search courses and related forms of intensified counselling for persons with difficulties in finding employment;

support of geographic mobility and similar costs in connection with job search and placement. In addition to the above programme costs, all administration costs of labour market agencies (at central and decentralised levels), including unemployment benefit agencies (even if these are separate institutions) as well as administrative costs arising from the pursuit of other labour market programmes are included.

2. Labour market training

Training measures undertaken for reasons of labour market policy, other than special programmes for youth and the disabled. The expenditures include both course costs and subsistence allowances to trainees. Subsidies to employers for enterprise training are also included, but not employers' own expenses.

a) Training for unemployed adults and those at risk
Job training programmes open mainly – though not always exclusively – for the unemployed and those at risk of losing their jobs, or other disadvantaged groups such as the poor (especially in the United States). Mostly in training centres, but often also in enterprises.

b) Training for employed adults
Training supported for reasons of labour market policy other than the need to help the unemployed and those at risk. Most frequently, grants to enterprises for staff training in general.

3. Youth measures

Including only special programmes for youth in the process of transition from school to work. Thus it does not cover young people's participation in programmes that are open to adults as well.

a) Measures for unemployed and disadvantaged youth
Remedial education, training or work practice offered to facilitate transition from school to work for disadvantaged youth. The principal target group usually consists of those who do not follow regular upper-secondary or vocational education and who are also unsuccessful in finding jobs.

b) Support of apprenticeship and related forms of general youth training
Covers many forms of training and work practice in enterprises for young people. Access is not restricted to persons with employment problems.

4. Subsidised employment

Targeted measures to promote or provide employment for unemployed persons and other groups defined according to labour market policy priorities (other than youth or the disabled).

a) Subsidies to regular employment in the private sector
Wage subsidies for the recruitment of targeted workers or, in some cases, for continued employment of persons whose jobs are at risk. Grants aiming primarily to cover enterprises' capital costs are not included, nor are general employment subsidies or subsidies paid for all workers in certain regions.

b) Support of unemployed persons starting enterprises
The support can consist of unemployment benefits or special grants.

c) Direct job creation (public or non-profit)
Temporary works and, in some cases, regular jobs in the public sector or in non-profit organisations, offered to unemployed persons.

5. Measures for the disabled

Only special programmes for the disabled are included. The category does not cover the total policy effort in support of the disabled.

a) Vocational rehabilitation
Ability testing, work adjustment measures and training other than ordinary labour market training.

b) Work for the disabled
Sheltered work and subsidies to regular employment.

6. Unemployment compensation

All forms of cash benefit to compensate for unemployment, except early retirement. In addition to unemployment insurance and assistance, this covers publicly-funded redundancy payments, compensation to workers whose employers go bankrupt, and special support of various groups such as construction workers laid off during bad weather.

7. Early retirement for labour market reasons

Only special schemes in which workers receive retirement pensions because they are out of work or because their jobs are released to the benefit of others. Disability pensions are not included. The programme expenditures depend largely on the extent to which early pensions are subsidised rather than funded within regular pension plans, e.g. by actuarially calculated reductions of the pensions.

B. COUNTRY TABLES ON LABOUR MARKET PROGRAMMES

Public expenditure in national currency 1985-1989,
and programme participants in the latest available year.

Source: National submissions to the OECD

Conventional signs

.. Data not available
- Nil or less than half of the last digit used

STANDARD PROGRAMME CATEGORIES

1. **Public employment services and administration**
2. **Labour market training**
   a) Training for unemployed adults and those at risk
   b) Training for employed adults
3. **Youth measures**
   a) Measures for unemployed and disadvantaged youth
   b) Support of apprenticeship and related forms of general youth training
4. **Subsidised employment**
   a) Subsidies to regular employment in the private sector
   b) Support of unemployed persons starting enterprises
   c) Direct job creation (public or non-profit)
5. **Measures for the disabled**
   a) Vocational rehabilitation
   b) Work for the disabled
6. **Unemployment compensation**
7. **Early retirement for labour market reasons**

Australia

Programme	1985-86 million A$	1986-87 million A$	1987-88 million A$	1988-89 million A$	1989-90 million A$	Participants starting 1987-88
Public employment services and administration	**273.7**	**291.6**	**312.3**	**323.9**	..	
Placement and information services	171.8	170.7	173.5	177.1	..	
Labour market and education analysis	10.5	11.1	9.6	13.7	..	
Other administration[a]	88.3	105.8	123.2	125.1	..	
Mobility assistance	3.1	4.0	4.6	3.9	..	
Job-search counselling and related training	—	—	1.4	4.1	48.0	
Labour market training	**40.2**	**71.6**	**79.3**	**185.7**	..	**36 000**
a) *Training for unemployed adults and those at risk*	*28.5*	*55.2*	*62.7*	*160.1*	..	*33 300*
Adult Training	18.5	27.8	29.5	72.6	..	26 800
Industry and Regional Assistance	0.9	12.3	14.4	22.7	..	1 300
Community Training	9.1	15.1	18.8	—	—	5 171
Skill Share[b]	—	—	—	64.7	90.2	—
b) *Training for employed adults*						
Skills Training	*11.7*	*16.4*	*16.6*	*25.6*	..	*2 800*
Youth measures	**157.4**	**176.1**	**209.4**	**204.1**	..	..
a) *Measures for unemployed and disadvantaged youth*	*66.6*	*66.3*	*78.2*	*43.3*		..
Special Trade Training[c]	19.6	18.9	16.8	14.8		5 560
Other	15.5	12.3	25.9	28.5		12 423
Community Youth Support	31.5	35.1	35.5	—		..
b) *Support of apprenticeship and related forms of general youth training*	*90.8*	*109.8*	*131.2*	*160.8*		*65 600*
Apprenticeships	88.7	96.2	102.6	120.1		55 415
Traineeship system[d]	2.1	13.6	28.6	40.7		10 166
Subsidised employment	**463.3**	**388.4**	**284.5**	**156.7**	**177.9**	**66 750**
a) *Subsidies to regular employment in the private sector*						
Jobstart[e]	*114.9*	*124.4*	*108.5*	*68.3*	*84.0*	*45 100*
b) *Support of unemployed persons starting enterprises*						
New Enterprise Incentive	—	—	*0.9*	*4.5*	*7.8*	*450*
c) *Direct job creation (public or non-profit)*	*348.4*	*264.0*	*175.1*	*83.9*	*86.1*	*21 200*
Community Employment	289.9	199.0	99.5	1.2	—	9 659
Community Volunteer Program	—	1.8	3.4	—	—	—
Labour market measures for Aboriginals[f]	58.5	63.2	72.2	82.7	86.1	11 579

Australia *(Cont'd)*

Programme	1985-86 million A$	1986-87 million A$	1987-88 million A$	1988-89 million A$	1989-90 million A$	Participants starting 1987-88
Measures for the disabled[g]			**97.2**	**112.6**	**119.1**	..
a) *Vocational rehabilitation*	..	..	*39.1*	*49.3*	*49.7*	*6 170*
b) *Work for the disabled*	..	..	*58.1*	*63.3*	*69.4*	..
Unemployment compensation	**3 122.0**	**3 454.0**	**3 374.9**	**3 284.3**	**3 356.8**	
Unemployment benefits	3 122.0	3 454.0	3 347.2	3 235.3	3 302.0	
Job-search allowance (for under 18-year-olds)	—	—	27.7	49.0	54.8	
Total	**4 056.6**	**4 381.7**	**4 357.6**	**4 267.3**	..	

Fiscal years from 1 July.

a) General administration of the Commonwealth Labour and Employment function plus administration of labour market programmes.
b) Replaces the programmes entitled Community Training, Community Youth Support and Community Volunteer Program.
c) Measures to complement regular apprentice training and support disadvantaged trainees.
d) For non-craft occupations.
e) For recruitment of long-term unemployed persons.
f) Including some elements of formal training.
g) Administered by the Department of Community Services and Health.

Austria

Programme	1985 million Sch.	1986 million Sch.	1987 million Sch.	1988 million Sch.	1989 million Sch.	Participants starting 1988
Public employment services and administration	**1 445**	**1 541**	**1 660**	**1 667**	**1 716**	
Employment authorities	1 430	1 523	1 640	1 656	1 704	
Mobility support	15	18	20	11	12	
Labour market training	**1 168**	**1 558**	**1 873**	**1 082**	**1 435**	**32 500**
a) *Training for unemployed adults and those at risk*						
Institutional training	1 045	1 433	1 644	1 034	1 333	28 406
Enterprise training	123	126	229	48	102	4 114
Youth measures	**392**	**405**	**371**	**189**	**167**	**10 100**
a) *Measures for unemployed and disadvantaged youth*	*392*	*405*	*371*	*189*	*167*	*10 100*
Subsidised employment	**453**	**682**	**820**	**499**	**580**	**11 000**
a) *Subsidies to regular employment in the private sector*	*345*	*294*	*313*	*141*	*138*	*7 900*
Counter-cyclical subsidies	22	94	94	29	62	824
Winter supports (mainly building)	157	49	43	50	66	6 679
Subsidised recruitment of hard-to-place persons	66	83	83	34	10	400
Restructuring	100	67	93	28	—	—
c) *Direct job creation (public or non-profit)*	*108*	*388*	*507*	*358*	*442*	*3 066*
Measures for the disabled	**311**	**466**	**546**	**567**	**700**	**12 100**
a) *Vocational rehabilitation*						
Training and mobility support[a]	*112*	*220*	*275*	*263*	*370*	*9 554*
b) *Work for the disabled*	*199*	*246*	*271*	*304*	*330*	*2 566*
Unemployment compensation	**11 156**	**12 317**	**13 923**	**13 914**	**13 616**	
Unemployment benefits	7 014	7 811	8 744	8 261	8 003	
Means-tested assistance	2 381	2 700	3 260	3 542	3 364	
Bad-weather compensation (for building)	395	365	403	312	304	
Social security contributions paid for the unemployed	1 366	1 441	1 515	1 799	1 944	
Early retirement for labour market reasons[b]	**1 735**	**2 000**	**2 481**	**2 556**	**2 231**	
Total	**16 660**	**18 969**	**21 673**	**20 474**	**20 444**	

a) Excluding expenditure by social security institutions.
b) "Special support" (*Sonderunterstützung*) for displaced workers plus advanced pension payments by the unemployment insurance.

Belgium

Programme	1985 million BF	1986 million BF	1987 million BF	1988 million BF	Participants starting 1988
Public employment services and administration	**8118**	**8489**	**9011**	**10044**	
Employment offices	4466	4836	5325	5737	
Programme administration	300	300	334	355	
Unemployment insurance administration	3352	3352	3352	3952	
Labour market training	**5389**	**6150**	**6654**	**7631**	**69600**
a) *Training for unemployed adults and those at risk*[a]	..	..	*6412*	..	*67355*
Training centres				..	61560
Enterprise training					5795
b) *Training for employed adults*					
Training for creation, extension or réconversion of enterprises	..	..	*242*	..	*2239*
Youth measures	..	..	**1113**	**1028**	..
a) *Measures for unemployed and disadvantaged youth*	..	..	*1113*	*1028*	
Subsidised employment	**37500**	**42800**	**40299**	**36881**	..
a) *Subsidies to regular employment in the private sector*	—	—	*2282*	*3419*	..
Recruitment of the unemployed in small and medium firms	—	—	574	503	
Unemployed workers replacing workers on leave	—	—	1708	2916	
b) *Support of unemployed persons starting enterprises*[b]	..	..	*891*	*692*	*1600*
c) *Direct job creation (public or non-profit)*	*37500*	*42800*	*37126*	*32770*	..
Subsidised regular public sector jobs[c]	—	—	11961	11952	
Temporary-job schemes	37500	42800	23680	20165	
Other	—	—	1485	653	
Measures for the disabled	**7124**	**7661**	**8543**	**10224**	..
a) *Vocational rehabilitation*	*2743*	*2990*	*3332*	..	
b) *Work for the disabled*	*4381*	*4671*	*5211*	..	
Unemployment compensation	**121468**	**123240**	**127048**	**125057**	
Early retirement for labour market reasons	**41288**	**42500**	**42650**	**44674**	
Total	**220887**	**230840**	**235318**	**235539**	

a) Mostly in training centres, run predominantly by the public employment agency. Unemployment benefits paid to trainees are included.

b) A loan of currently BF 569000 per approved project. In addition, the job-search requirement for unemployment benefits is waived during six months.

c) Local governments get subsidies for regular employment contracts signed with persons who have been unemployed for at least six months. This scheme was started in 1987 to replace three temporary-job schemes (temporary work for the unemployed, special temporary work for the very long-term unemployed, and "third circuit work" with churches and other non-profit organisations) which are being phased out.

Canada

Programme	1985-86 million C$	1986-87 million C$	1987-88 million C$	1988-89 million C$	1989-90 million C$	Participants starting 1988-89
Public employment services and administration	**1 171**	**1 218**	**1 224**	**1 249**		
National Employment Service	263	243	231	255	..	
Programme management and joint services	122	143	150	124	..	
Canadian Jobs Strategy (CJS) administration[a]	157	156	148	168	166	
Unemployment benefit administration	339	366	384	397	..	
Corporate and special services	290	310	311	306	..	
Labour market training	**1 635**	**1 770**	**1 652**	**1 616**	**1 736**	**241 000**
a) *Training for unemployed adults and those at risk*	..	*1 570*	*1 381*	*1 332*	*1 438*	*154 900*
Job Development (mainly for the long-term unemployed)[a]	..	834	597	481	474	65 700
Job Entry (for women)[a]	..	228	364	370	408	52 000
Skill Investment[a]	..	49	66	81	96	32 500
Community Futures[a]	..	64	71	118	150	4 700
Unemployment benefits during training	235	237	224	244	244	..
Other[a]	..	162	59	38	66	..
b) *Training for employed adults*	..	*200*	*271*	*285*	*300*	*86 200*
Skill Shortages[a]	..	185	235	246	255	86 200
Innovations[a]	..	15	36	39	43	—
Youth measures	**160**	**118**	**123**	**128**	**134**	**85 200**
a) *Measures for unemployed and disadvantaged youth*						
Job Entry Summer (Challenge)[a]	*160*	*118*	*123*	*128*	*134*	*85 200*
Subsidised employment	**109**	**96**	**87**	**102**	**110**	**22 700**
c) *Direct job creation (public or non-profit)*						
Unemployment benefits in work projects	*109*	*96*	*87*	*102*	*110*	*22 700*
Unemployment compensation[b]	**9 095**	**9 440**	**9 180**	**9 596**	..	
Total	**12 170**	**12 646**	**12 266**	**12 691**	..	

Fiscal years from 1 April.

a) The Canadian Jobs Strategy (CJS) consists of several programmes, here classified according to their approximate targets. Each of them can include various activities; the emphasis is on training but some forms of wage subsidies are also available.

b) Including benefits for the fishing industry and compensation for part-time unemployment due to work sharing. Excluding benefits for those aged 65 and over and for participants in training and job creation.

Denmark

Programme	1986 million DKr	1987 million DKr	1988 million DKr	1989 million DKr	Participants starting 1988
Public employment services and administration	**560**	**642**	**713**	**697**	
Local employment services	382	431	478	474	
Administration[a]	171	204	227	218	
Mobility support	7	7	8	5	
Labour market training	**3 244**	**3 250**	**3 524**	**4 004**	**192 000**
a) *Training for unemployed adults and those at risk*	*1 721*	*1 592*	*1 703*	*1 904*	*38 685*
Enterprise training[b]	1 519	1 342	1 403	1 604	34 335
Education allowance[c]	202	250	300	300	4 350
b) *Training for employed adults*					
Short courses[d]	*1 523*	*1 658*	*1 821*	*2 100*	*153 000*
Youth measures	**1 552**	**1 675**	**1 860**	**1 781**	**50 000**
a) *Measures for unemployed and disadvantaged youth*					
Education allowance[e]	21	23	21	30	300
Introductory work experience courses[f]	171	177	169	162	11 000
Work practice[g]	360	367	410	409	39 000 (Work practice and Measures by municipalities)
Measures by municipalities[h]	1 000	1 108	1 260	1 180	
Subsidised employment	**93**	**128**	**160**	**240**	
b) *Support of unemployed persons starting enterprises*	*68*	*125*	*160*	*240*	*900*
c) *Direct job creation (public or non-profit)*	*25*	*3*	—	—	
Measures for the disabled	**1 640**	**1 846**	**2 231**	**2 418**	..
a) *Vocational rehabilitation*	*920*	*989*	*1 289*	*1 362*	*39 000*
b) *Work for the disabled*	*720*	*857*	*942*	*1 056*	..
Training and sheltered employment	258	297	315	331	
Sheltered workshops	462	560	627	725	
Unemployment compensation	**17 648**	**18 719**	**21 288**	**24 650**	
Early retirement for labour market reasons	**8 376**	**8 689**	**9 064**	**9 700**	
Total	**33 113**	**34 949**	**38 840**	**43 490**	

a) The Ministry of Labour, the Directorate of Labour, the Directorate for Unemployment Insurance, the Directorate for Adult Vocational training, the Council for Vocational and Educational Guidance, the Industrial Court and the Public Conciliator.
b) The *Arbejdstilbud* (job offer) scheme, in which long-term unemployed persons are offered enterprise training for 7-9 months.
c) For up to 2 years of remedial education and training.
d) Labour market training centres give courses for semi-skilled jobs (about two-thirds of the cases) and further training. Most courses last about two weeks. Some 50-60 per cent of the trainees have jobs. The expenses include allowances paid to trainees.
e) Paid to unemployed youngsters for up to 2 years' education and training.
f) Courses in training centres lasting about 8 weeks.
g) Both regular jobs and direct job creation.
h) Measures of the same nature as "work practice". Municipalities are required by law to provide such jobs for unemployed youth.

Finland

Programme	1985 million Mk	1986 million Mk	1987 million Mk	1988 million Mk	1989 million Mk	Participants starting 1988
Public employment services and administration[a]	**265**	**339**	**387**	**437**	**487**	
Labour market training	**894**	**988**	**1012**	**1168**	**1243**	**31700**
a) *Training for unemployed adults and those at risk*	*894*	*988*	*1012*	*1168*	*1243*	*31700*
Youth measures	**110**	**91**	**67**	**115**	**113**	**12500**
a) *Measures for unemployed and disadvantaged youth*	*82*	*62*	*38*	*84*	*80*	*10200*
Work introduction slots	82	62	38	34	25	4600
Recruitment subsidies	—	—	—	50	55	5600
b) *Support of apprenticeship and related forms of general youth training*						
Summer jobs for students	*28*	*29*	*29*	*31*	*33*	*2300*
Subsidised employment	**1420**	**1460**	**1694**	**2196**	**2365**	**82000**
a) *Subsidies to regular employment in the private sector*	*157*	*125*	*169*	*139*	*158*	*10500*
b) *Support of unemployed persons starting enterprises*	*—*	*22*	*71*	*132*	*121*	*3600*
c) *Direct job creation (public or non-profit)*	*1263*	*1313*	*1454*	*1925*	*2086*	*68000*
Public works to promote employment	470	475	457	406	370	3000
Temporary state jobs	247	300	324	446	736	12700
Grants to municipalities for temporary work	546	538	673	1073	980	52400
Measures for the disabled	**300**	**339**	**391**	**552**	**677**	..
a) *Vocational rehabilitation*	..	*107*	*131*	*168*	*197*	*13500*
b) *Work for the disabled*	..	*232*	*260*	*384*	*480*	..
Employment subsidy	..	32	25	62	82	2600
Sheltered work	..	200	235	322	398	..
Unemployment compensation	**2927**	**3531**	**3676**	**3588**	**3120**	
Basic and wage-related benefits	2710	3254	3445	3372	2900	
Redundancy payments	129	186	138	122	100	
Bankruptcy pay guarantee	88	91	93	94	120	
Early retirement for labour market reasons	**1553**	**2016**	**2414**	**2616**	**2666**	
Total	**7469**	**8764**	**9641**	**10672**	**10671**	

a) Including mobility support.

France

Programme	1985 million FF	1986 million FF	1987 million FF	1988 million FF	Participants starting 1988
Public employment services and administration	**6 200**	**6 479**	**6 669**	**6 760**	
Employment agency (ANPE)[a]	2 563	2 661	2 728	2 915	
Administration of income maintenance programme (ASSEDIC)[b]	3 637	3 818	3 941	3 846	
Labour market training	**11 955**	**13 672**	**14 051**	**17 714**	**950 000**
a) *Training for unemployed adults and those at risk*	*10 481*	*12 012*	*12 066*	*15 510*	*570 000*
Courses and training allowances for the unemployed[c]	10 024	11 618	11 801	15 360	550 000
Training of employed persons during restructuring[d]	457	394	265	150	16 870
b) *Training for employed adults*	*1 474*	*1 660*	*1 985*	*2 204*	*380 000*
Funded by the central government[e]	523	761	909	1 066	200 000
Funded by regions	951	899	1 076	1 138	180 000
Youth measures	**7 900**	**11 795**	**16 401**	**14 331**	**1 035 000**
a) *Measures for unemployed and disadvantaged youth*	*2 478*	*4 224*	*4 104*	*3 890*	*335 000*
Temporary jobs[f]	2 478	3 977	3 728	3 525	335 000
Counselling	..	247	376	365	—
b) *Support of apprenticeship and related forms of general youth training*	*5 421*	*7 571*	*12 297*	*10 441*	*700 000*
Reduced social security contributions for apprenticeship	1 056	1 150	1 294	1 453	132 600
Ditto for other training or recruitment[g]	—	2 288	5 597	2 574	—
Alternance training grants[h]	2 980	2 579	1 993	2 635	272 200
Grants to working-life insertion jobs[i]	360	1 267	3 357	3 779	297 554
Grants to employment-training contracts	1 025	288	56	—	—
Subsidised employment	**2 815**	**2 996**	**2 837**	**2 982**	..
a) *Subsidies to regular employment in the private sector*	*773*	*726*	*590*	*702*	..
Reduced social security contributions[j]	—	—	20	259	19 700
Grants connected with reduced working time	333	254	91	63	1 000
Local initiatives and experimental activities	308	189	81	87	18 000
Other	132	283	398	293	
b) *Support of unemployed persons starting enterprises*	*2 042*	*2 256*	*1 976*	*1 769*	*55 600*
c) *Direct job creation (public or non-profit)*[k]	—	*14*	*271*	*511*	*39 000*
Measures for the disabled	**2 403**	**2 658**	**2 849**	**3 035**	..
b) *Work for the disabled*	*2 403*	*2 658*	*2 849*	*3 035*	

France *(Cont'd)*

Programme	1985 million FF	1986 million FF	1987 million FF	1988 million FF	Participants starting 1988
Unemployment compensation	**56 430**	**62 906**	**70 240**	**75 372**	
Insurance and assistance	54 115	60 756	68 820	74 357	
Partial unemployment benefits	839	542	391	204	
Compensation to dockers for temporary unemployment	126	138	128	98	
Bad-weather compensation to construction workers	1 166	1 240	500	300	
Industrial restructuring compensation	184	230	401	413	
Early retirement for labour market reasons	**55 289**	**51 204**	**45 712**	**41 296**	
Income maintenance[l]	28 333	24 865	20 833	17 898	
Special FNE payments	9 448	11 552	12 810	13 797	
"Solidarity contracts"	9 986	7 050	3 928	1 274	
Other	7 502	7 737	8 141	8 327	
Total	**142 993**	**151 710**	**158 759**	**161 490**	

a) *Agence Nationale pour l'Emploi.*
b) *Associations pour l'Emploi dans l'Industrie et le Commerce,* representing employers and employees, organised nationally in a body called UNEDIC.
c) Most courses are organised by the adult training agency *(Association pour la Formation Professionnelle des Adultes,* AFPA). Also included are expenses by the *Fonds National de l'Emploi* (FNE), the *Fonds de la Formation Professionnelle et de la Promotion Sociale* (FFPPS), and regional authorities.
d) Enterprises facing technological or economic restructuring can sign agreements with the FNE, which then subsidises training.
e) Mainly the FFPPS.
f) *Travaux d'utilité collective,* in which 16-25 year-olds out of work since more than a year are employed for 3 to 12 months by local governments and non-profit organisations.
g) Social security contributions are waived during alternance training (*contrats d'adaptation* or *contrats de qualification*). Before 1988 they were also reduced by 25 or 50 per cent in certain other cases.
h) Public outlays for training and subsistence allowances, available to 16-24 year-olds.
i) *Stages d'initiation à la vie professionnelle* (SIVP). Public outlays for subsistence allowances and, to a lesser extent, training costs.
j) A reduction by 50 per cent for long-term unemployed persons who are hired or given alternance training.
k) Three schemes called *Programmes d'insertion locale* (PIL), *Programmes locaux d'insertion en faveur des femmes isolées* (PLIF), and *Compléments locaux de ressources* (CLR).
l) Paid by the *Association pour la Structure Financière,* which derives one-third of its fund from the central government and two-thirds from UNEDIC (see note *b*).

Germany

Programme	1985 million DM	1986 million DM	1987 million DM	1988 million DM	1989 million DM	Participants starting 1988
Public employment services and administration	**3 832**	**4 324**	**4 635**	**5 084**	**5 212**	
Central and local offices	3 682	4 106	4 420	4 707	5 050	
Mobility support, etc.[a]	150	218	215	377	162	
Labour market training	**3 643**	**4 652**	**5 940**	**6 753**	**6 585**	**649 000**
a) *Training for unemployed adults and those at risk*	..	*3 583*	*4 589*	*5 347*	*5 185*	*421 100*
Further training[b]	..	2 219	2 774	2 931	..	221 000
Retraining	..	849	1 106	1 200	..	65 700
Introductory training in enterprises	..	285	384	373	370	51 200
German for resettlers	212	230	325	844	850	83 200
b) *Training for employed adults*						
Further training[b]	..	*1 069*	*1 352*	*1 406*	*1 400*	*228 000*
Youth measures	**878**	**1 002**	**1 160**	**1 096**	**1 060**	**248 300**
a) *Measures for unemployed and disadvantaged youth*	..	*747*	*857*	*833*	*940*	*113 100*
Preparatory measures[c]	..	334	345	379	401	67 800
Measures for disadvantaged youth[d]	251	310	388	391	463	36 000
Remedial education[e]	81	103	124	63	76	9 300
b) *Support of apprenticeship and related forms of general youth training*						
Apprentice allowance (except for preparatory measures, see above)[f]	..	*255*	*303*	*263*	*120*	*135 200*
Subsidised employment	**3 068**	**3 742**	**4 177**	**4 842**	**4 383**	..
a) *Subsidies to regular employment in the private sector*	*891*	*1 007*	*949*	*1 231*	*1 098*	..
Recruitment subsidies[g]	210	306	323	377	162	39 800
Winter building subsidies[h]	642	620	461	573	496	..
Wage subsidy for the aged long-term unemployed	39	81	165	281	440	7 300
b) *Support of unemployed persons starting enterprises*	—	*25*	*51*	*180*	*75*	*10 000*
c) *Direct job creation (public or non-profit)*[i]	*2 177*	*2 710*	*3 177*	*3 431*	*3 210*	*142 000*
Measures for the disabled	**3 541**	**3 875**	**4 322**	**4 800**	**4 900**	..
a) *Vocational rehabilitation (by the employment authorities)*	*1 900*	*2 130*	*2 445*	*2 821*	*2 939*	*187 900*
b) *Work for the disabled*	*1 583*	*1 745*	*1 877*	*2 000*	*2 000*	..
Sheltered workshops (outlays by the social authorities)	1 142	1 308	1 453	1 500	..	
Measures for seriously disabled persons[j]	441	437	424	450	..	

Germany *(Cont'd)*

Programme	1985 million DM	1986 million DM	1987 million DM	1988 million DM	1989 million DM	Participants starting 1988
Unemployment compensation	**25 769**	**25 281**	**26 828**	**28 262**	**28 994**	
Insurance	14 085	14 022	15 293	18 054	18 258	
Assistance	9 126	9 160	9 030	8 447	8 770	
Short-time work compensation	1 228	880	1 240	978	780	
Bad-weather compensation for construction workers	772	691	778	448	809	
Bankruptcy compensation	558	528	487	335	377	
Early retirement for labour market reasons	**95**	**289**	**394**	**477**	**473**	
Full retirement	95	289	394	477	401	
Part-time retirement	—	—	—	—	72	
Total	**40 826**	**43 165**	**47 460**	**51 314**	**51 607**	

a) Grants to individuals within the programme "Incentives to take up work" *(Förderung der Arbeitsaufnahme).* Recruitment subsidies to employers ("integration assistance", see note *g)* are not included here.

b) The costs of further training have been distributed between the two sub-categories "training for unemployed adults and those at risk" and "training for employed adults" according to the approximate distribution of participants. This is likely to imply some overestimation of the proportion of outlays attributable to employed workers.

c) Vocationally preparatory measures *(Berufsvorbereitende Massnahmen),* often leading to regular apprentice training.

d) This programme *(Benachteiligtenprogramm)* supports apprentices who are socially disadvantaged or of foreign origin. It provides training in special schools or in enterprises receiving special support.

e) Education allowances *(Bildungsbeihilfen)* paid to unemployed youth for remedial general or vocational education.

f) The apprentice allowance *(Berufsausbildungsbeihilfe)* is a means-tested income supplement, paid mainly when the allowances paid by employers (i.e. the "wages") are below certain limits. The item does not cover preparatory measures (see note *c).*

g) "Integration assistance" *(Eingliederungsbeihilfe),* a recruitment subsidy paid to employers under the programme "Incentives to take up work".

h) Promotion of building productivity by winter grants *(Wintergeld)* and certain additional subsidies.

i) "General measures to create work" *(Allgemeine Massnahmen zur Arbeitsbeschaffung),* targeting the long-term unemployed and certain other categories of hard-to-place persons. The works are organised by local bodies. The subsidies are paid mainly by labour market authorities but also by certain other public sources.

j) Funded by a levy on employers who do not employ as many seriously disabled persons as is required by law *(Schwerbehindertengesetz).*

Greece

Programme	1985 million Dr	1986 million Dr	1987 million Dr	1988 million Dr	Participants starting 1988
Public employment services and administration	**3 000**	**3 600**	**4 587**	**5 056**	
Labour market training	**6 431**	**8 321**	**13 001**	**16 010**	**23 600**
a) *Training for unemployed adults and those at risk*					
Training centres	..	..	..	*1 340*	*3 000*
b) *Training for employed adults*					
Enterprise training	..	..	..	*14 670*	*20 600*
Youth measures	**1 871**	**2 672**	**2 700**	**2 860**	**11 000**
b) *Support of apprenticeship and related forms of general youth training*	*1 871*	*2 672*	*2 700*	*2 860*	*11 000*
Subsidised employment	**3 887**	**6 125**	**10 550**	**14 850**	**68 100**
a) *Subsidies to regular employment in the private sector*	..	..	..	*9 750*	*39 000*
b) *Support of unemployed persons starting enterprises*	..	..	..	*3 500*	*11 600*
c) *Direct job creation (public or non-profit)*	..	..	..	*1 600*	*17 500*
Measures for the disabled	**691**	**1 187**	**1 695**	**1 320**	**1 820**
a) *Vocational rehabilitation*	..	..	..	*750*	*750*
b) *Work for the disabled*					
Employment subsidies	..	..	..	*570*	*1 070*
Unemployment compensation	**20 191**	**25 334**	**26 100**	**29 250**	
Total	**36 071**	**47 239**	**58 633**	**69 346**	

Ireland

Programme	1985 million Ir£	1986 million Ir£	1987 million Ir£	1988 million Ir£	Participants starting 1988
Public employment services and administration	**25.7**	**28.7**	**32.9**	**31.7**	
The employment agency[a]	5.6	6.3	7.9	7.0	
Department of Employment, overheads	6.8	7.5	7.4	7.8	
Employment exchanges administering unemployment benefits	13.2	14.9	17.6	16.9	
Labour market training	**116.9**	**110.6**	**107.5**	**120.0**	**38 750**
a) *Training for unemployed adults and those at risk*					
Vocational courses[b]	*75.2*	*68.0*	*66.7*	*81.7*	*18 212*
b) *Training for employed adults*	*41.7*	*42.6*	*40.7*	*38.3*	*20 540*
Enterprise training	20.0	20.8	21.0	21.4	7 400
New industry training grants[c]	20.0	20.0	17.6	14.0	8 000
Tourism[d]	1.7	1.8	2.1	2.9	5 140
Youth measures	**83.1**	**76.7**	**93.8**	**85.9**	**38 700**
a) *Measures for unemployed and disadvantaged youth*	*61.8*	*57.4*	*75.4*	*67.6*	*31 200*
Training workshops, etc.[e]	27.3	26.1	29.7	21.3	9 783
Teamwork (temporary work)	8.5	5.3	4.6	5.4	1 197
Graduate placement programme	—	—	1.1	0.9	193
Vocational preparation and training programme[f]	26.0	26.0	40.0	40.0	20 000
b) *Support of apprenticeship and related forms of general youth training*	*21.3*	*19.4*	*18.4*	*18.3*	*7 550*
Apprentice training[g]	17.8	15.7	14.5	14.3	1 824
Tourism training[h]	2.5	2.6	2.8	2.9	2 230
Farm training[i]	1.0	1.1	1.1	1.1	3 500
Subsidised employment	**33.8**	**64.4**	**65.7**	**61.3**	**16 200**
a) *Subsidies to regular jobs in the private sector*					
Employment Incentive[j]	*4.1*	*6.0*	*6.0*	*3.0*	*3 269*
b) *Subsidies to unemployed persons starting enterprises*	*13.6*	*14.5*	*10.4*	*7.4*	*2 720*
Enterprise Scheme	12.1	11.3	6.8	5.4	
Community Enterprise, etc.	1.5	3.2	3.6	2.0	
c) *Direct job creation (public or non-profit)*	*16.1*	*43.9*	*49.3*	*50.9*	*10 200*
Social employment	7.2	39.8	43.5	48.9	10 200
Other	8.9	4.1	5.8	2.0	..
Unemployment compensation	**655.0**	**696.5**	**715.6**	**704.3**	
Insurance and assistance	627.5	665.0	685.6	677.1	
Redundancy payments	27.5	31.5	30.0	27.2	
Total	**915**	**977**	**1 015**	**1 003**	

a) Three earlier agencies [Industrial Training Authority (AnCO), National Manpower Service and Youth Employment Agency] were merged into a new authority known as an Foras Aiseanna Saothar (FAS).
b) Specific Employable Skills (courses in centres), Building on Experience (alternance training with centres and enterprises), Enterprise Courses (for self-employment) and Local Training Initiatives. FAS capital and overhead costs are included except insofar as they pertain to employment services.
c) Paid by the Industrial Development Authority.
d) The Industry Training division of the Council for Education, Recruitment and Training for the Hotel, Catering and Tourism Industries (CERT).
e) The Community Youth Training, Training Workshops, Skills Foundation and special projects.
f) Courses for unemployed school-leavers provided by education authorities.
g) Most apprentices follow first-year courses in public training centres.
h) School-based courses organised by CERT (see note *d)*.
i) Organised by an agency called an Chomhairle Oiluna Talmhaiochta (ACOT).
j) For recruitment of the long-term unemployed.

Italy

Programme	1985 billion L	1986 billion L	1987 billion L	1988 billion L	Participants starting 1987
Public employment services and administration[a]	**628**	**875**	**777**	**850**	
Labour market training	**459**	**158**	**139**	**347**	..
a) *Training for unemployed adults and those at risk*					
"Labour mobility fund"	164	46	67	29	
"Fondo di rotazione"	272	—	—	318	
Other	23	112	72	—	
Youth measures	**2 572**	**5 139**	**6 598**	**7 441**	..
a) *Measures for unemployed and disadvantaged youth*	*1 772*	*2 439*	*2 598*	*2 838*	..
Training funded by the European Social Fund[b]	795	811	953	909	
Training organised by regions	857	863	870	1 000	
Recruitment subsidy[c]	—	285	285	80	
Restoration of cultural assets[d]	—	300	300	—	
Support of young people starting enterprises in the Mezzogiorno[e]	120	180	190	349	
Public works[f]	—	—	—	500	
b) *Support of apprenticeship and related forms of general youth training*	*800*	*2 700*	*4 000*	*4 603*	..
Apprenticeship[g]	—	1 500	1 700	1 803	..
Employment-training contracts[h]	800	1 200	2 300	2 800	164 000
Unemployment compensation	**6 134**	**5 084**	**4 820**	**4 292**	
Regular benefits	766	102	86	1 154	
Special benefits	840	1 533	1 627	806	
Cassa Integrazione Guadagni	4 528	3 449	3 107	2 332	
Early retirement for labour market reasons	**2 303**	**2 678**	**3 137**	**3 509**	
Total	**12 096**	**13 934**	**15 471**	**16 439**	

a) The central and peripheral offices of the Ministry of Labour.
b) Largely enterprise training, mainly for young people with employment problems but also for long-term unemployed adults. Part of the money is spent by regions, while part is centrally administered and part is paid directly to enterprises.
c) Law No. 113/86. For long-term unemployed youth.
d) Law No. 41/86 art. 15. For young unemployed persons with high educational qualifications.
e) Law No. 44/86.
f) Law No. 67/88 art. 23.
g) A reduction of social security contributions.
h) Law No. 863/84. An incentive for employers to hire and give approved training to people under 30. About two-thirds of the estimated expenses are paid by the central government and the remainder by regions.

Japan

Programme	1987-88 billion Y	1988-89 billion Y	1989-80 billion Y	Participants starting 1988-89
Public employment services and administration[a]	..	..	..	
Estimated running costs	..	..	..	
Special measures	9.8	12.2	13.5	
Labour market training	**98.2**	**105.7**	**111.2**	..
a) *Training for unemployed adults and those at risk*				
Vocational reconversion measures[b]	*8.9*	..	..	..
b) *Training for employed adults*	*89.3*	*105.7*	*111.2*	..
Promotion of technological change	17.7	31.1	30.7	..
Public vocational training	51.5	53.1	56.6	397 000
Vocational training in the private sector[c]	16.3	17.5	20.0	154 000
Other	3.8	3.9	3.9	..
Enterprise training				
Youth measures	**0.2**	..	..	..
Subsidised employment	**351.9**	**449.1**	**424.7**	..
a) *Subsidies to regular employment in the private sector*	*318.1*	*421.0*	*399.9*	
Employment-related measures to change the industrial structure	84.2	127.9	84.1	
Promotion of comprehensive regional employment measures	3.3	39.5	87.8	
Employment measures for persons who need special care	40.4	38.5	34.2	
Measures for aged workers	190.2	215.1	193.8	
c) *Direct job creation (public or non-profit)*	*33.8*	*28.0*	*24.7*	
Measures for the disabled	**29.9**	**39.6**	**39.9**	
Unemployment compensation	**1 426.7**	**1 424.8**	**1 395.5**	
Total (estimate)	**2 000**	**2 100**	**2 100**	

Fiscal years from 1 April.

a) Data not available. Total employment services and administration costs may be roughly estimated to be of the order of Y 100 billion.

b) After 1987-88 this category is inseparable from employment-related measures to change the industrial structure.

c) Approved training corresponding to public training but run by enterprises. These can get subsidies for training middle-aged and older employees. Only a small part of total enterprise training is covered by these subsidies.

Luxembourg

Programme	1985 million LF	1986 million LF	1987 million LF
Public employment services and administration	**93**	**101**	**106**
Labour market training			
a) *Training for unemployed adults and those at risk*	*4*	*75*	*39*
Youth measures	**218**	**185**	**217**
a) *Measures for unemployed and disadvantaged youth*	*154*	*127*	*162*
Vocational training and orientation	106	69	106
Temporary public sector work	48	58	56
b) *Support of apprenticeship and related forms of general youth training*	*63*	*59*	*54*
Subsidised employment	**275**	**160**	**162**
a) *Subsidies to regular employment in the private sector*			
Measures in the steel industry[a]	*271*	*148*	*149*
c) *Direct job creation (public or non-profit)*	*4*	*12*	*14*
Measures for the disabled	**598**	**614**	**616**
a) *Vocational rehabilitation*	*26*	*27*	*25*
b) *Work for the disabled*	*573*	*587*	*590*
Special measures for disabled steel industry workers	515	523	514
Re-hiring of the disabled	11	15	18
Sheltered workshops	47	49	58
Unemployment compensation	**647**	**643**	**701**
Full unemployment	478	471	503
Partial unemployment	22	22	27
Accident and bad-weather unemployment	135	141	156
Wage guarantee for bankruptcies	11	9	15
Early retirement for labour market reasons	**1 527**	**1 446**	**1 659**
Steel industry	1 527	1 446	1 638
General system	—	—	21
Total	**3 362**	**3 224**	**3 500**

a) Subsidies for special activities of general interest, organised for redundant workers as an alternative to dismissal.

Netherlands

Programme[a]	1985 million Gld	1986 million Gld	1987 million Gld	1988 million Gld	1989 million Gld	Participants starting 1989
Public employment services and administration[b]	**336**	**324**	**315**	**377**	**431**	
Labour market training	**840**	**888**	**913**	**1 035**	**960**	**140 000**
a) *Training for unemployed adults and those at risk*	*840*	*886*	*906*	*1 028*	*942*	*140 000*
Adult vocational training centres (CVV)	49	80	103	113	101	13 000
Framework regulation (various forms of training) (KRS)	..	181	173	238	175	59 000
Primary vocational adult education (PBVE)	..	18	20	23	27	17 500
Vocational guidance and training centres (CBB)	36	37	39	48	42	3 300
Information technology courses (IIG, PION)	—	5	16	23	10	2 000
Industry sectoral training (BBS)	—	—	—	—	25	—
Measures by municipalities[c]	20	20	30	30	30	30 000
Regional plans (PCG, BRP)	120	145	125	128	108	11 500
Unemployment benefits during training (estimate)	400	400	400	425	425	—
b) *Training for employed adults*	—	*3*	*7*	*7*	*18*	..
Information technology training (ACSI, NIIO)	—	3	7	7	3	—
Support of training in small firms (SSW)	—	—	—	—	15	..
Youth measures	**169**	**195**	**238**	**298**	**369**	**62 000**
a) *Measures for unemployed and disadvantaged youth*	*3*	*9*	*32*	*81*	*118*	*14 000*
Temporary municipality work (GWJ "Work Guarantee")	—	—	7	51	70	9 000
Work practice slots (JOB)	3	9	25	30	49	4 500
b) *Support of apprenticeship and related forms of general youth training* (BVJ)	*166*	*186*	*206*	*217*	*251*	*48 000*
Subsidised employment	**237**	**367**	**267**	**185**	**356**	**23 000**
a) *Subsidies to regular employment in the private sector*	*70*	*47*	*84*	*118*	*168*	*16 000*
Support of work insertion for the long-term unemployed (MOA)[d]	70	46	28	23	25	5 000
Subsidy plus lower social security contributions for the very long-term unemployed (MLW, Vermeend/Moor Act)[e]	—	1	56	94	133	10 300
Grants to jobless persons taking low-paid jobs (PALL)	—	—	—	2	10	600
c) *Direct job creation (public or non-profit)*	*168*	*320*	*183*	*67*	*188*	*6 700*
Special works (WVM)	118	45	30	23	21	700
Construction works (TPP)	50	175	100	—	—	—
Work practice for the long-term unemployed	—	—	—	—	100	6 000
Other	—	100	54	44	67	..

Netherlands *(Cont'd)*

Programme	1985 million Gld	1986 million Gld	1987 million Gld	1988 million Gld	1989 million Gld	Participants starting 1989
Measures for the disabled	**3085**	**3026**	**3025**	**3103**	**3155**	**6400**
b) *Work for the disabled* (WSW)	3085	3026	3025	3103	3155	6400
Unemployment compensation	**12712**	**12816**	**12144**	**12087**	**12305**	
Total	**17379**	**17615**	**16902**	**17084**	**17575**	

a) The acronyms represent programme names in Dutch.
b) Administration of unemployment benefits is not included.
c) Various measures for which municipalities receive money from the unemployment insurance (Art. 36 WWV).
d) A subsidy lasting six months for recruitment of persons out of work for more than a year.
e) Estimated cost of waiving social security contributions plus a training subsidy for recruitment of persons out of work for more than 3 years.

New Zealand

Programme	1985-86 million NZ$	1986-87 million NZ$	1987-88 million NZ$	1988-89 million NZ$	Participants starting 1987-88
Public employment services and administration[a]	**23**	**35**	**43**	**53**	
Department of Labour	23	31	39	..	
Other ministries[b]	1	1	2	..	
Mobility support	—	4	3	1	
Labour market training	**40**	**127**	**265**	**320**	**70 000**
a) *Training for unemployed adults and those at risk*					
ACCESS[c]	40	127	225	250	
Maori ACCESS	—	—	40	70	
Youth measures	**5**	**5**	**5**	**8**	**7 546**
a) *Measures for unemployed and disadvantaged youth*					
Conservation Corps	—	—	—	*3*	—
b) *Support of apprenticeship and related forms of general youth training*	*5*	*5*	*5*	*5*	*7 546*
Subsidised employment	**278**	**182**	**62**	**135**	..
a) *Subsidies to regular employment in the private sector*[d]	*20*	*25*	*46*	*135*	..
c) *Direct job creation (public or non-profit)*	*258*	*158*	*17*	—	
Measures for the disabled					
a) *Vocational rehabilitation*	*7*	*8*	*10*	*9*	*22 300 (1986-87)*
Rehabilitation League	7	8	10	9	22 300 (1986-87)
Unemployment compensation	**291**	**460**	**632**	..	
Total	**643**	**818**	**1 018**	..	

Fiscal years from 1 April.
a) Excluding unemployment benefit administration.
b) Parts of the Department of Maori Affairs and the Department of Internal Affairs.
c) For both youth and adult job-seekers. About half the training is delivered by community organisations, about 25 per cent by training institutes and the rest by employers or other bodies.
d) Various kinds of partly subsidised employment.

Norway

Programme	1985 million NKr	1986 million NKr	1987 million NKr	1988 million NKr	1989 million NKr	Participants starting 1989
Public employment services and administration	**625**	**675**	**681**	**700**	**905**	
The employment agency[a]	567	616	624	652	858	
Mobility support	33	34	32	22	19	
Related social security administration	25	25	25	25	27	
Labour market training	**542**	**460**	**333**	**386**	**1 767**	**60 000**
a) *Training for unemployed adults and those at risk*						
Adult training centres	448	411	317	368	1 463	
Enterprise training grants	94	49	16	18	304	
Youth measures	**234**	**228**	**115**	**140**	**682**	..
a) *Measures for unemployed and disadvantaged youth*						
Subsidised work practice	162	149	72	100	480	11 000
Apprenticeships in the public sector	51	64	38	26	40	500
Wage subsidies	21	15	5	14	162	..
Subsidised employment	**1 028**	**255**	**50**	**79**	**992**	..
a) *Subsidies to regular employment in the private sector*[b]	*83*	*82*	*34*	*50*	*146*	
b) *Support of unemployed persons starting enterprises*	—	—	—	*8*	*22*	
c) *Direct job creation (public or non-profit)*	*945*	*173*	*16*	*21*	*824*	
Measures for the disabled	**888**	**954**	**1 016**	**1 059**	**1 189**	**11 000**
a) *Vocational rehabilitation*	*77*	*82*	*92*	*81*	*113*	..
b) *Work for the disabled*	*811*	*872*	*924*	*978*	*1 076*	..
Sheltered workshops	510	556	598	643	690	
Other public sector jobs	161	172	183	185	210	
Wage subsidies	140	144	142	150	176	
Unemployment compensation	**2 518**	**1 971**	**1 998**	**3 176**	**6 368**	
Total	**5 835**	**4 543**	**4 193**	**5 540**	**11 903**	

a) The Directorate of Labour *(Arbeidsdirektorat),* county labour offices, local employment offices and institutes for vocational rehabilitation.

b) For the long-term unemployed and the elderly and for promotion of sex equality, and as from 1989 also for youth.

Portugal

Programme	1986 million Esc	1987 million Esc	1988 million Esc	1989 million Esc	Participants starting 1988
Employment services and administration[a]	**3 328**	**4 621**	**5 626**	**7 891**	
Labour market training	**9 268**	**8 966**	**12 122**	**13 876**	**75 000**
a) *Training for unemployed adults and those at risk*	—	*296*	*788*	*1 398*	*2 310*
Job training in the area of cultural heritage conservation	—	268	680	1 153	810
Complementary training for ex-trainees	—	28	108	245	1 500
b) *Training for employed adults*	*9 268*	*8 670*	*11 334*	*12 478*	*73 000*
Support of co-operative training centres	2 518	3 337	4 923	5 100	18 564
Support of other co-operative vocational training	5 862	4 343	4 772	4 522	50 000
Public training centres[b]	888	990	1 639	2 856	4 824
Youth measures	**1 889**	**4 249**	**6 078**	**6 923**	**23 100**
a) *Measures for unemployed and disadvantaged youth*	*1 222*	*2 768*	*3 409*	*1 028*	*16 800*
Temporary work	1 186	2 723	3 337	887	16 700
Work and training for unemployed youngsters without qualifications	36	45	72	141	100
b) *Support of apprenticeship and related forms of general youth training*	*668*	*1 480*	*2 669*	*5 895*	*6 300*
Support of apprenticeship	555	1 381	2 511	5 385	6 000
Training and work insertion for white-collar workers	113	99	158	510	300
Subsidised employment	**1 711**	**5 005**	**6 343**	**7 712**	**26 060**
a) *Subsidies to regular employment in the private sector*	*149*	*1 587*	*2 164*	*3 439*	*4 900*
Recruitment subsidies[c]	149	1 132	811	1 327	3 850
Local initiatives[d]	—	455	1 353	2 112	1 052
b) *Support of unemployed persons starting enterprises*	*349*	*820*	*983*	*1 075*	*4 442*
Grants (including grants to artisan work)[e]	263	734	941	992	3 730
Use of unemployment benefits	86	86	42	83	712
c) *Direct job creation (public or non-profit)*	*1 213*	*2 598*	*3 196*	*3 198*	*16 716*
Temporary works	973	2 390	2 969	..	13 426
Measures for seasonal workers	240	208	227	..	3 290

Portugal *(Cont'd)*

Programme	1986 million Esc	1987 million Esc	1988 million Esc	1989 million Esc	Participants starting 1988
Measures for the disabled	**1 838**	**1 129**	**1 938**	**3 130**	**4 155**
a) *Vocational rehabilitation*	*1 258*	*1 040*	*1 798*	*2 755*	*3 680*
Vocational preparation and training	1 000	970	1 601	2 350	3 400
Support of work integration	258	70	197	405	280
b) *Work for the disabled*	*580*	*89*	*140*	*375*	*475*
Unemployment compensation	**17 907**	**19 351**	**18 313**	**20 282**	
Total	**35 941**	**43 321**	**50 420**	**59 814**	

a) The Institute for employment and vocational training *(Instituto do Emprego e formaçao profissional).* The *investments* of this institute are not included; they amounted to about Esc 8 000 million in 1987 including new training facilities.
b) Excluding investment costs (see note *a)*).
c) For permanent employment contracts concerning persons who are younger than 25 years or long-term unemployed.
d) The subsidy is highest for enterprises employing a high proportion of labour market entrants and unemployed people, but it is not paid exclusively for these.
e) Several programmes in support of enterprise startups and artisan work.

Spain

Programme	1985[a] million Ptas	1986[a] million Ptas	1987 million Ptas	1988 million Ptas	Participants starting 1987
Public employment services and administration	**27 240**	**24 450**	**27 980**	**34 200**	
Labour market training	**1 050**	**22 180**	**34 310**	**49 110**	**ca.200 000**
a) *Training for unemployed adults and those at risk*	*1 050*	*21 530*	*32 400*	*44 770*	*177 762*
For the long-term unemployed	1 050	9 340	14 770	17 390	50 914
For rural temporary workers	—	8 340	10 150	13 550	42 935
Industrial reconversion training	—	3 020	2 800	5 010	17 986
For returning emigrants	—	80	180	150	
Other	—	750	4 500	8 670	65 927
b) *Training for employed adults*	—	*650*	*1 910*	*4 340*	..
Training for new technologies in firms with less than 500 employees	—	110	900	2 440	13 453
Other	—	540	1 010	1 900	..
Youth measures	**14 970**	**62 490**	**81 040**	**78 880**	..
a) *Measures for unemployed and disadvantaged youth*	*14 970*	*52 860*	*70 750*	*71 030*	..
Training of unemployed under 25 years old	—	20 670	39 790	51 460	130 000
Grant for recruitment in regular jobs	—	13 070	12 100	5 100	118 500
Subsidised work practice	—	3 110	4 440	—	..
Transformation of work practice contracts into regular employment	—	560	420	150	..
Reduced social security contributions[b]	14 970	15 450	14 000	14 320	..
b) *Support of apprenticeship and related forms of general youth training*	—	*9 630*	*10 290*	*7 850*	..
Alternance training	—	9 630	8 440	5 140	6 164
Work practice for students	—	—	1 850	2 710	..
Subsidised employment	**57 230**	**116 410**	**121 840**	**142 530**	**387 500**
a) *Subsidies to regular employment in the private sector*	*5 040*	*12 340*	*7 030*	*8 970*	*18 400*
Grants for recruitment of the unemployed	3 980	6 920	100	2 180	—
Grants for recruitment of over 45 year-olds	—	600	1 350	2 520	10 535
Grants for recruitment of women in jobs where they are under-represented	—	290	330	310	510
Support of employment in worker co-operatives	1 060	2 440	2 810	3 300	6 894
Local initiatives	..	2 090	2 440	660	423
b) *Support of unemployed persons starting enterprises*[c]	*15 340*	*59 070*	*70 200*	*85 120*	*66 000*
c) *Direct job creation (public or non-profit)*	*36 850*	*45 020*	*44 610*	*48 440*	*303 125*
Temporary jobs[d]	27 590	39 920	39 260	39 940	292 900
Use of unemployment benefits for public works	9 260	5 100	5 350	8 500	10 225

Spain *(Cont'd)*

Programme	1985[a] million Ptas	1986[a] million Ptas	1987 million Ptas	1988 million Ptas	Participants starting 1987
Measures for the disabled	**1 000**	**2 470**	**4 380**	**3 120**	..
a) *Vocational rehabilitation*	—	*240*	*440*	*500*	..
b) Work for the disabled	*1 000*	*2 230*	*3 940*	*2 620*	*9 400*
Recruitment subsidy	—	640	2 290	2 620	3 469
Work integration[e]	1 000	1 590	1 650	—	5 917
Unemployment compensation	**806 890**	**820 070**	**882 330**	**923 480**	
Insurance	415 000	383 800	385 270	396 900	
Assistance	125 390	147 620	185 190	177 370	
Aid to temporary farm workers[f]	42 880	58 360	67 000	84 650	
Bankruptcy compensation, etc.	50 980	55 700	73 510	97 060	
Social security contributions paid for the unemployed	172 640	174 620	171 360	167 500	
Early retirement for labour market reasons	**7 590**	**4 490**	**13 400**	**13 560**	
In enterprises under restructuring	2 800	2 120	9 480	9 630	
In other enterprises in crisis	3 900	2 370	3 920	3 930	
Other	890	—	—	—	
Total	**915 970**	**1 052 560**	**1 165 280**	**1 244 880**	

a) The figures for 1985 and 1986 do not cover a special fund *(Fondo de Solidaridad para el Empleo)*, which operated training for about Ptas 16 billion and other activities for about Ptas 14 billion in the two years.
b) For unemployed under 26 years old and certain other categories of young workers.
c) Mainly use of unemployment benefits.
d) About two-thirds of spending and of the average employment was accounted for by work with local associations. These jobs lasted on average one month. The remaining jobs were with local and central governments and lasted about four months on average.
e) A subsidy to projects creating jobs, preferably but not necessarily on a permanent basis.
f) Mainly in Andalucia and Extremadura.

Sweden

Programme	1985-86 million SKr	1986-87 million SKr	1987-88 million SKr	1988-89 million SKr	1989-90 million SKr	Participants starting 1987-88
Public employment services and administration	**2 287**	**2 519**	**2 421**	**2 482**	**2 518**	
The employment agency[a]	1 696	1 936	1 972	2 031	2 050	
Unemployment insurance funds	200	200	270	320	320	
Mobility support	391	383	179	131	148	
Labour market training	**4 514**	**4 959**	**5 821**	**6 330**	**6 440**	**97 000**
a) *Training for unemployed adults and those at risk*	*4 514*	*4 959*	*5 658*	*6 111*	*6 240*	*76 000*
Course costs	2 358	2 271	2 517	2 667	2 840	
Subsistence allowances	2 156	2 688	3 141	3 444	3 400	
b) *Training for employed adults*						
Grants to enterprise training (e.g. for skill shortages)	—	—	*163*	*219*	*200*	*21 000*
Youth measures	**1 881**	**1 691**	**1 273**	**968**	**800**	..
a) *Measures for unemployed and disadvantaged youth*						
Schools' follow-up measures	220	223	224	266	..	..
"Youth teams"[b]	1 661	1 465	966	593	..	27 000
Work practice slots	—	3	83	109	..	..
Subsidised employment	**3 857**	**3 102**	**2 491**	**2 194**	**2 030**	..
a) *Subsidies to regular employment in the private sector*	*890*	*633*	*576*	*459*	*230*	..
Recruitment subsidies, etc.[c]	709	491	462	373	200	16 500
Support of jobs in the textile and apparel industry	181	142	114	86	30	..
b) *Support of unemployed persons starting enterprises*	*77*	*82*	*87*	*94*	*100*	*2 000*
c) *Direct job creation (public or non-profit)*	*2 890*	*2 387*	*1 828*	*1 641*	*1 700*	*36 000*
Temporary job creation	2 739	2 355	1 731	1 381	1 400	
Special regional measures	—	7	27	38	40	
Measures for the part-time unemployed	—	—	20	60	60	
Other	151	25	50	162	200	
Measures for the disabled	**6 524**	**7 475**	**8 036**	**8 738**	**9 235**	..
a) *Vocational rehabilitation*	*839*	*925*	*1 037*	*1 117*	*1 160*	..
Labour market institutes	705	789	868	972	1 000	18 600
Workplace adjustment grants	134	136	169	145	160	..
b) *Work for the disabled*	*5 685*	*6 550*	*6 999*	*7 621*	*8 075*	..
Wage subsidies	2 709	3 151	3 375	3 836	4 100	14 000
Sheltered public employment	99	295	349	352	375	..
Sheltered workshops	2 877	3 104	3 275	3 433	3 600	..

Sweden *(Cont'd)*

Programme	1985-86 million SKr	1986-87 million SKr	1987-88 million SKr	1988-89 million SKr	1989-90 million SKr	Participants starting 1987-88
Unemployment compensation	**6 758**	**7 546**	**7 461**	**6 819**	**7 400**	
Unemployment benefits	6 049	6 973	6 934	6 379	7 000	
Bankruptcy wage guarantee	709	573	527	440	400	
Early retirement for labour market reasons	**1 100**	**1 121**	**1 128**	**1 130**	**1 130**	
Total	**26 921**	**28 413**	**28 631**	**28 661**	**29 553**	

Fiscal years from 1 July.

a) The national labour market board *(Arbetsmarknadsstyrelsen,* AMS) and the county labour market boards *(Länsarbetsnämnder)* which run employment offices.

b) Work practice and job search for 18-20 year-olds.

c) For the long-term unemployed and other hard-to-place persons.

Switzerland

Programme	1985 million SF	1986 million SF	1987 million SF	1988 million SF	Participants starting 1988
Public employment services and administration	**177**	**177**	**181**	**184**	
Placement[a]	92	86	87	87	
Vocational guidance[a]	45	50	54	57	
Administration of unemployment benefits[b]	40	41	40	40	
Mobility support	0.4	0.4	0.4	0.4	
Labour market training	**30**	**33**	**34**	**35**	**8 400**
a) *Training for unemployed adults and those at risk*					
Course costs	8	9	9	10	—
Unemployment benefits paid during courses	8	8	9	9	6 400
Workplace training programmes	14	16	16	16	2 000
Subsidised employment	**2**	**2**	**2**	**3**	**360**
a) *Subsidies to regular employment in the private sector*					
Work insertion grants	*2*	*2*	*2*	*3*	*360*
Measures for the disabled	**187**	**210**	**222**	**242**	..
a) *Vocational rehabilitation*	*95*	*107*	*117*	*132*	
Training	79	89	97	108	
Special placement measures	16	18	20	24	
b) *Work for the disabled*					
Sheltered workshops	*92*	*103*	*105*	*110*	
Unemployment compensation	**644**	**558**	**576**	**500**	
Unemployment benefits (except during training)	447	386	376	361	
Short-time work benefits	28	22	44	39	
Bad-weather benefits	98	85	91	34	
Bankruptcy compensation	3	4	5	6	
Payments to other countries	24	17	21	24	
Social security contributions paid for the unemployed	44	43	39	36	
Total	**1 041**	**980**	**1 014**	**964**	

a) Mainly communal and cantonal expenditure.
b) Insurance funds and related administration by other bodies.

Turkey

Programme	1986 million TL	1987 million TL	1988 million TL	1989 million TL	Participants starting 1988
Public employment services and administration	**5 155**	**9 852**	**14 181**	**18 147**	
Labour market training	**9 250**	**22 580**	**31 663**	**72 000**	**646 500**
a) *Training for unemployed adults and those at risk*	..	..	..	..	*54 300*
b) *Training for employed adults*	..	..	..	..	*592 200*
People's training centres					471 860
Further training					120 324
Youth measures	**13 850**	**33 412**	**43 758**	**90 245**	**129 000**
b) *Support of apprenticeship and related forms of general youth training*	*13 850*	*33 412*	*43 758*	*90 245*	*129 000*
Subsidised employment	**27 560**	**39 206**	**55 247**	**74 950**	..
b) *Support of unemployed persons starting enterprises*	*27 560*	*39 206*	*55 247*	*74 950*	..
Measures for the disabled	**2 461**	**2 804**	**3 680**	**4 802**	**10 225**
a) *Vocational rehabilitation*	*2 461*	*2 804*	*3 680*	*4 802*	*10 225*
Total	**58 276**	**107 854**	**148 529**	**260 144**	

United Kingdom

Programme	1985-86 million £	1986-87 million £	1987-88 million £	1988-89 million £	1989-90 million £	Participants starting 1989-90
Public employment services and administration	**508**	**622**	**677**	**684**	**715**	
Job Centres	114	114	115	99	98	
Careers Service[a]	76	87	88	97	97	
"Restart" Programme for the long-term unemployed[b]	—	49	67	63	73	
Unemployment benefit administration	256	287	314	332	354	
Central services[c]	62	85	93	93	93	
Labour market training	**311**	**382**	**448**	**710**	**1 268**	..
a) *Training for unemployed adults and those at risk*						
Employment Training (and the older schemes it replaced)	..	*248*	*310*	*562*	*1 121*	*402 000*
b) *Training for employed adults*	*64*	*134*	*138*	*148*	*147*	..
Business Growth Through Training	..	24	26	27	27	117 000
Work-related Further Education	64	110	112	119	112	..
Enterprise in Higher Education	—	—	—	2	8	..
Youth measures	**915**	**999**	**1 086**	**1 147**	**1 164**	**403 000**
a) *Measures for unemployed and disadvantaged youth*	*56*	*52*	*40*	*31*	*28*	*6 800*
Community Industry[d]	24	25	25	25	28	6 800
New Workers Scheme	32	27	15	6	—	—
b) *Support of apprenticeship and related forms of general youth training*	*859*	*947*	*1 046*	*1 116*	*1 136*	*396 000*
Youth Training Scheme	818	875	988	1 027	1 015	280 000
Technical and Vocational Education Initiative[e]	41	72	58	88	117	80 000
"Compacts"[f]	—	—	—	1	4	36 000
Subsidised employment	**782**	**1 200**	**1 295**	**874**	**188**	
b) *Support of unemployed persons starting enterprises*[g]	*104*	*143*	*196*	*198*	*188*	*80 000*
c) *Direct job creation (public or non-profit)*	*678*	*1 057*	*1 099*	*676*	—	
Community Programme	667	1 043	1 085	664	—	
Voluntary Projects Programme	11	14	14	12	—	
Measures for the disabled	**116**	**104**	**110**	**121**	**134**	**37 000**
a) *Vocational rehabilitation* (including employment services)	*20*	*22*	*23*	*27*	*27*	*16 100*
b) *Work for the disabled*[h]	*96*	*82*	*87*	*94*	*107*	*20 655*

United Kingdom *(Cont'd)*

Programme	1985-86 million £	1986-87 million £	1987-88 million £	1988-89 million £	1989-90 million £	Participants starting 1989-90
Unemployment compensation	**7 304**	**7 537**	**6 751**	**5 459**	**4 813**	
Unemployment benefits	1 589	1 734	1 468	1 107	812	
Other income support[i]	5 371	5 556	5 202	4 283	3 928	
Redundancy Fund	344	247	81	69	73	
Early retirement for labour market reasons						
Job Release Scheme	**188**	**110**	**74**	**39**	**—**	
Total	**10 122**	**10 954**	**10 441**	**9 034**	**8 282**	

Fiscal years from 1 April.

a) Sponsored mainly by local authorities.
b) Including Jobclubs, Restart courses and Jobstart allowances.
c) Mainly policy planning and support functions.
d) Temporary work for disadvantaged 17-19 year-olds.
e) Stimulates the provision of technical and vocational education for 14-18 year-olds, including work experience, leading to nationally recognised qualifications.
f) A scheme run in co-operation with employers and schools to give young people training in enterprises.
g) The Enterprise Allowance Scheme.
h) Remploy, a company for sheltered work, plus jobs managed by local authorities.
i) Income Support replaced Supplementary Benefits in 1988. The figures include related housing benefits and rate (local tax) rebate for the unemployed.

United States

Programme	1985-86 million $	1986-87 million $	1987-88 million $	1988-89 million $	1989-90 million $	Participants starting 1987-88
Public employment services and administration	**2 900**	**2 850**	**2 985**	**2 994**	**2 851**	
Employment services[a]	875	796	808	795	790	
Veterans employment and training	115	126	137	159	163	
Work Incentive Program Grants[b]	202	126	192	190	—	
Administration[c]	1 708	1 802	1 848	1 850	1 898	
Labour market training	**4 896**	**5 020**	**5 080**	**5 133**	**5 169**	**7 800 000**
a) *Training for unemployed adults and those at risk*						
Training for the disadvantaged[d]	1 783	1 842	1 810	1 788	1 788	950 200
Vocational education (Perkins Act)[e]	2 813	2 805	2 796	2 848	2 819	6 585 000
Employment training for dislocated workers[f]	126	175	262	285	371	181 700
Emergency Veterans Job Training Act[g]	35	30	36	39	1	7 934
Trade Adjustment Assistance[h]	25	50	50	45	74	10 000
Measures for natives, migrants and seasonal farmworkers[i]	114	118	126	128	116	108 364
Youth measures	**1 397**	**1 288**	**1 420**	**1 426**	**1 497**	**868 000**
a) *Measures for unemployed and disadvantaged youth*	*1 385*	*1 276*	*1 407*	*1 412*	*1 483*	*772 600*
Summer Youth[j]	725	636	750	718	709	706 000
Job Corps[k]	660	640	657	694	774	66 600
b) *Support of apprenticeship and related forms of general youth training*						
National Apprenticeship Act[l]	*12*	*12*	*13*	*14*	*14*	*95 550*
Subsidised employment	**829**	**496**	**626**	**684**	**616**	**690 000**
a) *Subsidies to regular employment in the private sector*						
Targeted Job Tax Credit[m]	*517*	*160*	*295*	*340*	*280*	*600 000*
c) *Direct job creation (public or non-profit)*						
Senior Community Employment Program[n]	*312*	*336*	*331*	*344*	*336*	*90 000*
Measures for the disabled	**1 643**	**1 848**	**1 957**	**2 052**	**2 138**	**916 700**
a) *Vocational rehabilitation*						
For veterans[o]	103	106	112	107	108	24 700
Other[p]	1 540	1 742	1 845	1 945	2 030	892 000
Unemployment compensation	**23 927**	**23 325**	**20 966**	**19 357**	**20 112**	
Unemployment benefits	16 407	15 713	15 573	14 025	14 512	
AFDC/WIN family support[q]	7 400	7 400	5 200	5 200	5 390	
Trade adjustment allowance	120	212	193	132	210	
Total	**35 592**	**34 827**	**33 034**	**31 646**	**32 383**	

Fiscal years to 30 September.

a) The Wagner-Peyser Act of 1933, as amended. Primarily grants to state employment agencies to support total cost of job search and placement services to job-seekers, and recruitment and special technical services to employers. Also includes national activities.

b) Social Security Act Title IV. The Work Incentive (WIN) programme provides job services, training and public service employment to employable recipients of AFDC (Aid to Families with Dependent Children) who are 16 years or older. Includes 10 per cent matching state funds. For 1990, no WIN funds have been requested because this programme will be replaced by Job Opportunities and Basic Skills Training (JOBS), established by the 1988 Family Support Act. AFDC recipients with children over age 3 will henceforth be required to participate in training or education; spending data for this are not available.

c) Mainly costs of running unemployment insurance offices. Also includes various national activities such as information, research and evaluation.

d) Job Training Partnership Act (JTPA), Title II-A, provides grants to states for job-training measures targeted mainly on persons with low incomes. The programme includes classroom and on-the-job training as well as limited amounts of work experience and other activities. About 40 per cent of trainees are 16-21 year-olds.

e) Perkins Vocational Education Act, Title II-A. Federal grants towards secondary and post-secondary education for six specific target groups, often in vocational high school courses. State matching funds, estimated at approximately $2.3 billion per year, are included.

f) JTPA, Title III grants to states.

g) This programme is being phased out.

h) Trade Act of 1974 as amended in 1981, which funds retraining, job-search and removal costs for workers displaced by increased imports.

i) JTPA, Title IV-A.

j) JTPA, Title II-B, provides grants to states for minimum wage jobs and related services during the summer to economically disadvantaged youth aged 14 to 21.

k) JTPA, Title IV. Remedial education and job skills training for disadvantaged youth in 106 residential centres.

l) National Apprenticeship Act of 1937. Advice and technical assistance to employers.

m) Revenue Act of 1978 as amended. Outlay equivalent estimate including administration. The tax credit encourages employers to hire structurally unemployed workers.

n) JTPA, Title IX. Grants to states and national organisations for part-time community service work for unemployed low-income persons 55 years or older with poor job prospects.

o) Vocational rehabilitation for disabled veterans.

p) Vocational Rehabilitation Act of 1973 as amended. Estimate including 20 per cent matching state funds.

q) Estimate for 1989-90 (see note *b*).

WHERE TO OBTAIN OECD PUBLICATIONS
OÙ OBTENIR LES PUBLICATIONS DE L'OCDE

Argentina - Argentine
Carlos Hirsch S.R.L.
Galeria Güemes, Florida 165, 4° Piso
1333 Buenos Aires
Tel. 30.7122, 331.1787 y 331.2391
Telegram: Hirsch-Baires
Telex: 21112 UAPE-AR. Ref. s/2901
Telefax: (1)331-1787

Australia - Australie
D.A. Book (Aust.) Pty. Ltd.
648 Whitehorse Road (P.O. Box 163)
Vic. 3132 Tel. (03)873.4411
Telex: AA37911 DA BOOK
Telefax: (03)873.5679

Austria - Autriche
OECD Publications and Information Centre
4 Simrockstrasse
5300 Bonn (Germany) Tel. (0228)21.60.45
Telex: 8 86300 Bonn
Telefax: (0228)26.11.04

Gerold & Co.
Graben 31
Wien I Tel. (0222)533.50.14

Belgium - Belgique
Jean De Lannoy
Avenue du Roi 202
B-1060 Bruxelles
Tel. (02)538.51.69/538.08.41
Telex: 63220 Telefax: (02)538.08.41

Canada
Renouf Publishing Company Ltd.
1294 Algoma Road
Ottawa, Ont. K1B 3W8 Tel. (613)741.4333
Telex: 053-4783 Telefax: (613)741.5439
Stores:
61 Sparks Street
Ottawa, Ont. K1P 5R1 Tel. (613)238.8985
211 Yonge Street
Toronto, Ont. M5B 1M4 Tel. (416)363.3171

Federal Publications
165 University Avenue
Toronto, ON M5H 3B9 Tel. (416)581.1552
Telefax: (416)581.1743
Les Publications Fédérales
1185 rue de l'Université
Montréal, PQ H3B 1R7 Tel. (514)954-1633

Les Éditions La Liberté Inc.
3020 Chemin Sainte-Foy
Sainte-Foy, P.Q. G1X 3V6
Tel. (418)658.3763
Telefax: (418)658.3763

Denmark - Danemark
Munksgaard Export and Subscription Service
35, Norre Sogade, P.O. Box 2148
DK-1016 Kobenhavn K
Tel. (45 33)12.85.70
Telex: 19431 MUNKS DK
Telefax: (45 33)12.93.87

Finland - Finlande
Akateeminen Kirjakauppa
Keskuskatu 1, P.O. Box 128
00100 Helsinki Tel. (358 0)12141
Telex: 125080 Telefax: (358 0)121.4441

France
OECD/OCDE
Mail Orders/Commandes par correspondance:
2 rue André-Pascal
75775 Paris Cedex 16 Tel. (1)45.24.82.00
Bookshop/Librairie:
33, rue Octave-Feuillet
75016 Paris Tel. (1)45.24.81.67
(1)45.24.81.81
Telex: 620 160 OCDE
Telefax: (33-1)45.24.85.00

Librairie de l'Université
12a, rue Nazareth
13602 Aix-en-Provence Tel. 42.26.18.08

Germany - Allemagne
OECD Publications and Information Centre
4 Simrockstrasse
5300 Bonn Tel. (0228)21.60.45
Telex: 8 86300 Bonn
Telefax: (0228)26.11.04

Greece - Grèce
Librairie Kauffmann
28 rue du Stade
105 64 Athens Tel. 322.21.60
Telex: 218187 LIKA Gr

Hong Kong
Swindon Book Co. Ltd
13-15 Lock Road
Kowloon, Hong Kong Tel. 366.80.31
Telex: 50.441 SWIN HX
Telefax: 739.49.75

Iceland - Islande
Mal Mog Menning
Laugavegi 18, Postholf 392
121 Reykjavik Tel. 15199/24240

India - Inde
Oxford Book and Stationery Co.
Scindia House
New Delhi 110001 Tel. 331.5896/5308
Telex: 31 61990 AM IN
Telefax: (11)332.5993
17 Park Street
Calcutta 700016 Tel. 240832

Indonesia - Indonésie
Pdii-Lipi
P.O. Box 269/JKSMG/88
Jakarta12790 Tel. 583467
Telex: 62 875

Ireland - Irlande
TDC Publishers - Library Suppliers
12 North Frederick Street
Dublin 1 Tel. 744835/749677
Telex: 33530 TDCP EI Telefax : 748416

Italy - Italie
Libreria Commissionaria Sansoni
Via Benedetto Fortini, 120/10
Casella Post. 552
50125 Firenze Tel. (055)645415
Telex: 570466 Telefax: (39.55)641257
Via Bartolini 29
20155 Milano Tel. 365083
La diffusione delle pubblicazioni OCSE viene assicurata dalle principali librerie ed anche da:
Editrice e Libreria Herder
Piazza Montecitorio 120
00186 Roma Tel. 679.4628
Telex: NATEL I 621427

Libreria Hoepli
Via Hoepli 5
20121 Milano Tel. 865446
Telex: 31.33.95 Telefax: (39.2)805.2886

Libreria Scientifica
Dott. Lucio de Biasio "Aeiou"
Via Meravigli 16
20123 Milano Tel. 807679
Telefax: 800175

Japan- Japon
OECD Publications and Information Centre
Landic Akasaka Building
2-3-4 Akasaka, Minato-ku
Tokyo 107 Tel. 586.2016
Telefax: (81.3)584.7929

Korea - Corée
Kyobo Book Centre Co. Ltd.
P.O. Box 1658, Kwang Hwa Moon
Seoul Tel. (REP)730.78.91
Telefax: 735.0030

Malaysia/Singapore - Malaisie/Singapour
University of Malaya Co-operative Bookshop Ltd.
P.O. Box 1127, Jalan Pantai Baru 59100
Kuala Lumpur
Malaysia Tel. 756.5000/756.5425
Telefax: 757.3661

Information Publications Pte. Ltd.
Pei-Fu Industrial Building
24 New Industrial Road No. 02-06
Singapore 1953 Tel. 283.1786/283.1798
Telefax: 284.8875

Netherlands - Pays-Bas
SDU Uitgeverij
Christoffel Plantijnstraat 2
Postbus 20014
2500 EA's-Gravenhage Tel. (070)78.99.11
Voor bestellingen: Tel. (070)78.98.80
Telex: 32486 stdru Telefax: (070)47.63.51

New Zealand -Nouvelle-Zélande
Government Printing Office
Customer Services
P.O. Box 12-411
Freepost 10-050
Thorndon, Wellington
Tel. 0800 733-406 Telefax: 04 499-1733

Norway - Norvège
Narvesen Info Center - NIC
Bertrand Narvesens vei 2
P.O. Box 6125 Etterstad
0602 Oslo 6
Tel. (02)67.83.10/(02)68.40.20
Telex: 79668 NIC N Telefax: (02)68.19.01

Pakistan
Mirza Book Agency
65 Shahrah Quaid-E-Azam
Lahore 3 Tel. 66839
Telex: 44886 UBL PK. Attn: MIRZA BK

Portugal
Livraria Portugal
Rua do Carmo 70-74
1117 Lisboa Codex Tel. 347.49.82/3/4/5

Singapore/Malaysia Singapour/Malaisie
See "Malaysia/Singapore"
Voir "Malaisie/Singapour"

Spain - Espagne
Mundi-Prensa Libros S.A.
Castello 37, Apartado 1223
Madrid 28001 Tel. (91) 431.33.99
Telex: 49370 MPLI Telefax: 575.39.98

Libreria Internacional AEDOS
Consejo de Ciento 391
08009 -Barcelona Tel. (93) 301-86-15
Telefax: 575.39.98

Sweden - Suède
Fritzes Fackboksföretaget
Box 16356, S 103 27 STH
Regeringsgatan 12
DS Stockholm Tel. (08)23.89.00
Telex: 12387 Telefax: (08)20.50.21
Subscription Agency/Abonnements:
Wennergren-Williams AB
Box 30004
104 25 Stockholm Tel. (08)54.12.00
Telex: 19937 Telefax: (08)50.82.86

Switzerland - Suisse
OECD Publications and Information Centre
4 Simrockstrasse
5300 Bonn (Germany) Tel. (0228)21.60.45
Telex: 8 86300 Bonn
Telefax: (0228)26.11.04

Librairie Payot
6 rue Grenus
1211 Genève 11 Tel. (022)731.89.50
Telex: 28356

Maditec S.A.
Ch. des Palettes 4
1020 Renens/Lausanne Tel. (021)635.08.65
Telefax: (021)635.07.80

United Nations Bookshop/Librairie des Nations-Unies
Palais des Nations
1211 Genève 10
Tel. (022)734.60.11 (ext. 48.72)
Telex: 289696 (Attn: Sales)
Telefax: (022)733.98.79

Taïwan - Formose
Good Faith Worldwide Int'l. Co. Ltd.
9th Floor, No. 118, Sec. 2
Chung Hsiao E. Road
Taipei Tel. 391.7396/391.7397
Telefax: (02) 394.9176

Thailand - Thalande
Suksit Siam Co. Ltd.
1715 Rama IV Road, Samyan
Bangkok 5 Tel. 251.1630

Turkey - Turquie
Kültur Yayinlari Is-Türk Ltd. Sti.
Atatürk Bulvari No. 191/Kat. 21
Kavaklidere/Ankara Tel. 25.07.60
Dolmabahce Cad. No. 29
Besiktas/Istanbul Tel. 160.71.88
Telex: 43482B

United Kingdom - Royaume-Uni
H.M. Stationery Office
Gen. enquiries Tel. (071) 873 0011
Postal orders only:
P.O. Box 276, London SW8 5DT
Personal Callers HMSO Bookshop
49 High Holborn, London WC1V 6HB
Telex: 297138 Telefax: 071.873.8463
Branches at: Belfast, Birmingham, Bristol, Edinburgh, Manchester

United States - États-Unis
OECD Publications and Information Centre
2001 L Street N.W., Suite 700
Washington, D.C. 20036-4095
Tel. (202)785.6323
Telex: 440245 WASHINGTON D.C.
Telefax: (202)785.0350

Venezuela
Libreria del Este
Avda F. Miranda 52, Aptdo. 60337
Edificio Galipan
Caracas 106
Tel. 951.1705/951.2307/951.1297
Telegram: Libreste Caracas

Yugoslavia - Yougoslavie
Jugoslovenska Knjiga
Knez Mihajlova 2, P.O. Box 36
Beograd Tel. 621.992
Telex: 12466 jk bgd

Orders and inquiries from countries where Distributors have not yet been appointed should be sent to: OECD Publications Service, 2 rue André-Pascal, 75775 Paris Cedex 16.

Les commandes provenant de pays où l'OCDE n'a pas encore désigné de distributeur devraient être adressées à : OCDE, Service des Publications, 2, rue André-Pascal, 75775 Paris Cedex 16.

OECD PUBLICATIONS, 2 rue André-Pascal, 75775 PARIS CEDEX 16
PRINTED IN FRANCE
(81 90 01 1) ISBN 92-64-13363-1 - No. 45167 1990